Novell NetWare® on Command

Developed by New Riders Publishing

Text by

Drew Heywood

and

Danny Kusnierz

New Riders Publishing,
Carmel, Indiana

Novell NetWare on Command
by Drew Heywood and Danny Kusnierz

Published by:

New Riders Publishing
11711 N. College Ave., Suite 140
Carmel, IN 46032

Printed in the United States of America 1 2 3 4 5 6 7 8 9 0

Library of Congress Cataloging-in-Publication Data

Kusnierz, Danny, 1960-
Novell NetWare on Command / by Danny Kusnierz.
    p. cm.
Includes Index.
ISBN 1-56205-0011-7 : $19.95
1. Operating systems (Computers) 2. NetWare (Computer file)
I. Title.
QA76.76.063K87 1991
005.7'0369—dc20 91-33254 CIP

Publisher
David P. Ewing

Acquisitions Editor
Brad Koch

Managing Editor
Tim Huddleston

Series Director
Cheri Robinson

Editors
Peter Kuhns
Nancy Sixsmith
Rob Tidrow

Technical Editor
David Trout

Editorial Secretary
Karen Opal

Indexed by
Jeanne Clark

Production
Brad Chinn
Michelle Cleary
Brook Farling
Audra Hershman
Michele Laseau
Laurie Lee
Juli Pavey
Caroline Roop
Linda Seifert
Bruce Steed
Susan VandeWalle
Phil Worthington

Trademark Acknowledgments

Warning and Disclaimer

Table of Contents

2 SECURITY

5 PRINTING 153

Introduction

Perhaps the majority of local area network (LAN) administrators take on the task in addition to other assignments. The administrator may be the local PC expert, or may simply be the person in the department who is most comfortable with DOS and Lotus 1-2-3. The new administrator must move quickly from managing single-user PCs to managing a powerful, multiuser environment.

This book assists you in the day-to-day activities of administering a Novell NetWare local area network server without distracting you with descriptions of tasks that are either very technical or rarely performed. Even if you are an experienced administrator, you should find this book helpful for answering questions that are not covered in NetWare references.

When you receive your copy of NetWare, you also receive an imposing amount of documentation. The NetWare documentation contains references to the commands that are available in the NetWare environment. Although these references are complete and highly accurate, it is often difficult to identify which information from all the topics an administrator needs to know.

Managing a NetWare server involves two separate skill sets: those of configuring and installing the server hardware and software, and those of establishing and managing the user environment. Because the installation process is complicated by many variables such as the specific hardware that is being supported, you may find it best to have a NetWare expert complete the configuration and installation. After the server is up and running, however, many of the skills required for installation fall into disuse. Almost any user who is armed with a reasonably sized set of NetWare skills and who is comfortable with DOS is capable of performing most day-to-day tasks.

New NetWare system administrators must identify a suitable configuration for the server that makes administration as painless as possible. Even if a configuration plan is at hand, it is not always apparent how the many utilities and commands should be used to make that configuration a reality. Ordinarily, this process involves considerable trial-and-error along with intense study of the command references.

This book isolates the essential tasks for managing a NetWare server on a daily basis. It takes you from the jobs you must perform on a new server to suitable approaches for setting up user accounts and installing applications. It assists you in designing a LAN server configuration that is reliable, responsive to user requirements, and maintainable with a reasonable degree of effort.

Versions of NetWare

Novell NetWare has been through many revisions since its initial release. Most recently, Novell has spawned two series of NetWare products.

NetWare 3.11 is the current flagship. Because the 3.x versions of NetWare require a server equipped with at least an 80386 processor, this series is frequently referred to as 386 NetWare. The 3.x versions of NetWare are a complete revision of the older 2.x series, but are designed to keep much of the same command environment while taking advantage of the power available in the 80386 microprocessor. You can alter many features of NetWare 3.11 while the server is up and users are logged in, features that require halting a 2.x server for maintenance. The major changes in NetWare 3.x are in the areas of installation and configuration, and most of the same tools and techniques are still used for managing applications and user accounts.

NetWare Version 2.2 is the most recent release of the 2.x series, which is sometimes referred to as NetWare 286 because all members of the series can run on 80286-based microcomputers. Netware 2.2 is available in versions that support as few as 10 and as many as 100 users. Novell has positioned Version 2.2 to consolidate the NetWare 2.x product line (consisting of Versions 2.0a through 2.15) with the ELS NetWare product, which has been discontinued.

Netware Version 2.2 improves significantly on earlier 286 versions of NetWare. It is easier to configure and reconfigure. Version 2.2 also incorporates Novell's latest thinking on user and group rights and on file and directory flags. Rights and flags are defined similarly in Versions 2.2 and 3.11, although Version 3.11 extends rights in several ways.

This book would need to expand considerably to present all of the alternative methods needed to manage the various versions of NetWare. At least four distinct installation programs can be found in different products: ELSGEN in ELS NetWare, NETGEN in the Netware 2.1x series, INSTALL.EXE in Netware 2.2, and the INSTALL NetWare loadable module in Netware 3.x. Because most new installations utilize new versions of NetWare, and because most organizations benefit from upgrading older NetWare versions to one of the current releases, this book concentrates on describing procedures in terms of NetWare Versions 2.2 and 3.11.

How This Book is Organized

Each chapter presents tasks in a specific area. Whenever possible, the chapters are sorted in the order that you might need to use the information when configuring a new server. You probably will want to set up your volume and directory structures, for example, before you add users and groups.

The chapters are as follows:

- **Chapter 1: Disk and File Management**. This chapter describes the manner in which NetWare organizes disk storage into volumes, and the ways in which you can use subdirectories to efficiently manage the large-capacity storage devices that are increasingly typical on network servers. The essential characteristics of NetWare files are discussed, along with the techniques you use to copy them and to control their behaviors with NetWare attributes. Finally, the problem of storage management is addressed, with helpful techniques for managing file growth on servers.

- **Chapter 2: Security**. The data on a network server usually represents a considerable investment. The greater the value of the data, the more significant the issue of security becomes. The concepts of users and groups are introduced, along with the procedures for controlling user and group access to network resources.

- **Chapter 3: Workstations**. The workstation is as significant a part of a user's LAN environment as the server. Proper configuration of the workstation has a crucial effect on the reliability and friendliness of the user's LAN activities.

- **Chapter 4: Server Configuration**. Server configuration goes far beyond setting up the directories and volumes. Proper construction of login scripts is essential for controlling the LAN's user environment. Support for diskless workstations may be required. Workstations not equipped with hard drives may need to have access to DOS files that reside on the network server. Applications must be installed so that they behave properly in a multiuser environment.

- **Chapter 5: Printing**. Sooner or later, most LAN resources must produce printed output. Configuration issues for local and remote printers are discussed. Methods of configuring print queues and connecting them to printers also are described.

- **Chapter 6: Communications**. NetWare supports several communication methods between users. This chapter describes SEND messages and gives background on the NetWare Message Handling System.

- **Chapter 7: Server Monitoring**. Eventually, most servers experience performance problems. NetWare provides several tools that you can use to monitor servers, anticipate problems, and diagnose problems after they occur. NetWare also provides system administrators with tools for improving the performance of NetWare resources.

Each chapter is organized into two major sections. First a concepts section gives you background information. Then a tasks section goes through specific tasks in tutorial fashion.

From time to time, information boxes expand on the concepts presented in the tasks or discuss side issues that are raised by the task activities.

Icons

To help you focus on specific features that are of interest to you, *NetWare On Command* uses icons to indicate areas of interest. Underneath each task heading, you see a bar with four icons. The highlighted symbols apply to the task. The icons represent the following:

The Supervisor icon marks tasks that must be or are ordinarily performed by a supervisor.

The User icon indicates tasks that users can perform, provided the supervisor grants suitable privileges.

The Console icon identifies tasks that you must perform at a system console.

The Workstation icon identifies tasks that you can perform from any workstation.

Within each task section, you may see additional icons. These icons help you identify information that pertains to specific NetWare versions, tips to speed NetWare operations, and cautions to help you avoid costly mistakes. These icons are as follows:

 The NetWare 2.2 icon marks discussion that pertains specifically to Netware Version 2.2.

 The NetWare 3.11 icon identifies sections that are specific to Netware 3.11.

The Tip icon designates helpful information to speed your learning process of NetWare.

The Caution icon warns you of potential problems.

Presentation Conventions

NetWare uses both command-line and menu utilities to facilitate system management. If both approaches offer a way to complete a given task, both methods are presented. So that instructions can be presented clearly, certain typographical conventions are followed when describing the steps in a task.

Command-Line Utilities

NetWare documentation relies heavily on syntax diagrams to present the various options available with a command. The *syntax* of a command is simply the set of rules for constructing a proper command line, just as the syntax of a sentence consists of the grammatical rules for constructing an English sentence.

The most complex syntax diagrams can be hard to decipher because NetWare often permits several options in constructing a functionally equivalent command line. The tasks in this book present various examples of command usage to illustrate the ways in which you can structure a particular command. When a syntax diagram is presented, it follows Novell's conventions.

A distinctive typeface is used to identify commands you type or text you see on your computer screen. Here is an example of a command line as it will appear:

```
NCOPY PS1/SYS:HOME/DSMITH/*.* C:/TEMP /S
```

For consistency, commands that appear in the body of a paragraph are presented in the same typeface.

Although NetWare usually does not require that you enter commands in upper-, lower-, or mixed case, uppercase is used in all examples unless case is significant.

You frequently need to press specific keys to accomplish tasks. You may be instructed to press the Enter, F1, Ins, or Esc keys. The Enter key may not be specified in all examples. When a command line example is presented, it is assumed that you press Enter after completing the line.

Using Menu Utilities

NetWare relies heavily on menu utilities such as FILER and SYSCON. The operation of NetWare menu utilities is highly consistent, and you soon access menu features instinctively.

Starting a Menu Utility

To start a menu utility, enter the utility name at the DOS prompt.

Selecting a Menu Option

To *select* a menu option, you highlight the option and then press Enter. You will not be explicitly asked to press Enter each time.

Menu options appear in **bold**, both in task lists and in the bodies of paragraphs. Capitalization will be the same as the text in the menu.

Entering Directory Path

To enter a directory path, use one of the following methods:

1. Type the path name in the field provided, using the Backspace, Del, and arrow keys as needed to edit the text.

2. Select the path from a series of selection windows by following these procedures:

   - Press Backspace to erase the portions of the path that you want to discard.

   - Press Ins. A series of selection boxes is displayed that contains all valid choices for the current path.

   - Select an option from each successive box until the the desired path is displayed.

   - Press Esc to terminate the selection process.

   - Press Enter to accept the completed path.

Selecting Items from a List

To select items from a list, you can select several items before you press Enter. If you want to add several users to a group, for example, you can highlight each name and press F5. After you select all users, you can press Enter. Pressing F5 toggles the selection so that you can cancel a selection by highlighting it and pressing F5 a second time.

Quitting a NetWare Utility

To quit a NetWare menu utility, simply press Esc enough times to get to the box that asks you whether you want to quit and select the **Yes** option.

1

DISK AND FILE MANAGEMENT

Before much can be done on a server, its disk storage must be organized. The total storage capacity of the server is allocated to volumes, directories, and subdirectories so that you can store files in an efficient and organized manner. Then you must establish methods for finding and using particular files among the many files on the server.

This chapter explores disk and file management, including the following concepts:

- How do you organize a server's hard drives into volumes and directories?

- How do you use drive maps to facilitate access to files?

- How do you use file and directory attributes to control the way files are used?

- How can system administrators use NDIR to monitor storage of large numbers of files?

- How can system administrators limit directory size?

Key Concepts

Before examining the commands and procedures presented in this chapter, you must have an understanding of the following terms:

- Volumes

- Directories and subdirectories

- DOS path

- File and directory attributes

- Drive mapping

Discussion of these concepts builds on your knowledge of DOS to establish a foundation for understanding the ways in which NetWare manages disk storage.

Volumes

A *volume* is a named subdivision of the disk storage capacity of a server. Every NetWare server has at least one volume, which must be named SYS:. You can create other volumes, such as APPS: for applications or HOME: to hold users' personal files. Ordinarily, you will want to define additional volumes.

Volumes are organized in *blocks*. NetWare's standard size for a block is 4K (4 kilobytes or 4096 bytes). Space for files is allocated by whole blocks, which means that a 1-byte file requires 4096 bytes of disk space for storage; a 4100-byte file requires 8192 bytes of disk space.

System memory (RAM) works faster than disk drives, and NetWare keeps several tables in system memory to speed access to files. System memory that mirrors disk storage information in this way is called a *cache*. A substantial part of a NetWare server's memory is devoted to disk-cache services.

As you configure a server, you must make compromises. Setting up smaller blocks makes small files more economical to store but requires more server memory; 2K blocks have twice the memory overhead of the standard 4K blocks.

2.2 Under NetWare 286, volumes are limited to 255M and must be located on a single physical hard disk. You use almost the same process to create volumes in the various versions of Netware 286, although the utilities differ in name and detail of use. This book refers to INSTALL, which supersedes NETGEN (Netware 2.01 and Netware 2.1x), and ELSGEN (ELS Netware Level II).

Although you can reinstall NetWare and change the sizes of volumes, you erase all data from the volume. Make a tape backup of the volume you want to reorganize, therefore, so that the files can be restored. Because you cannot redefine volumes easily, the most effective strategy with Netware 286 is to keep volumes as large as possible and use directories to subdivide the volumes.

3.11 With Netware 386, volumes can be quite large. In fact, a volume can span several physical disk drives. In addition to support for vastly greater storage capacity, an important advantage of Netware 386 is the capability to increase the sizes of volumes. The NetWare 386 INSTALL loadable module enables you to add new segments of the current or of other disk drives to a volume. Once added, however, the segments cannot be removed without deleting the entire volume and rebuilding it from tape backups.

Novell recommends that volumes spanning multiple physical drives be *mirrored*. Mirroring is a technique of configuring two hard drives to contain identical information. If one drive fails, the information remains available on the mirrored drive. Once a volume spans multiple drives, a file can be spread across several drives. Failure of any one drive can damage the file. If you plan to set up such large volumes, you should read about disk mirroring in the NetWare manuals.

Because Netware 386 makes it easy for you to add segments to volumes, you can subdivide your main drive into SYS:, APPS:, and HOME: volumes. You can reserve part of the disk space to add to volumes that become filled to near capacity. This approach eliminates one level in your subdirectory names.

Directories and Subdirectories

NetWare uses directories and subdirectories in much the same manner as DOS to subdivide large disks into manageable units. Directories can contain files, but also can contain other directories, referred to as *subdirectories*. The most common method of depicting directories and subdirectories employs a tree, much like an inverted family tree. To further this analogy, a directory that contains another directory is frequently referred to as a *parent* directory and the subdirectory is referred to as a *child* *directory*.

NetWare directory names can include a server name and a volume name in the position DOS uses to indicate a volume letter. Most NetWare commands accept a directory path like the following:

```
FS1/APPS:LOTUS\123R3.1
```

In this example,

FS1/	Refers to the file server name
APPS:	Refers to a volume on the server
LOTUS\123R3.1	Refers to an application subdirectory

Depending on your defaults, part or all of this path specification can be omitted. If your current default directory is FS1/APPS:, you can refer to the 123R3.1 subdirectory in a NetWare command simply as:

```
\LOTUS\123R3.1
```

DOS always requires a backslash (\) to separate directories from subdirectories in a path. NetWare, however, accepts either a forward slash (/) or a backslash (\). Novell documentation alternates between use of backslash and forward slashes as directory separators. In at least one situation involving the NCOPY command, however, the use of forward slashes can cause problems. That situation is examined later in this chapter.

Because the backslash always works, it is used in all examples of directory separators in this book, whether they present DOS or NetWare commands. You may want to adopt the same practice.

Either type of slash can separate the server name from the volume name in a NetWare path. Both of the following examples are acceptable:

```
PS1/SYS:PUBLIC
PS1\SYS:PUBLIC
```

Because the server name/volume name component is unique to NetWare, this book standardizes the forward slash in that role.

 In NetWare, as in DOS, it is helpful to display the current directory on the command line. If you don't have a PATH statement in your AUTOEXEC.BAT file, you can add the following:

```
PROMPT $P$G
```

If your current directory is F:\PUBLIC, the preceding command makes your command line prompt look like this:

```
F:\PUBLIC>
```

Drive Maps

NetWare volumes can be much larger than typical DOS volumes, frequently containing over one billion bytes (one gigabyte or 1G). NetWare uses *drive maps* to reduce the confusion you may have in accessing specific volumes and directories. Mapping enables you to substitute lettered drives for complete directory paths.

Standard maps substitute a drive letter for a directory path. Suppose that drive H: is mapped to your home directory, which has the complete directory path of FS2/SYS:HOME\JSMITH. You can switch to your home directory simply by typing

    H:

If your prompt displays the current directory, it resembles this:

    H:\HOME\JSMITH>

Root maps differ from standard maps. Root maps make the mapped drive behave as though it were at the root of a volume. If drive H: is root mapped to JSMITH's home directory and drive H: is current, the prompt looks like this:

    H:\>

Even though a \HOME directory exists, you can't reach it from drive H. Consider the following dialog:

    H:\>**CD \HOME**
    Invalid Directory
    H:\>**CD ..**
    Invalid Directory

In the first example, DOS is fully convinced that a \HOME directory does not exist on drive H:. The second example uses .., which is DOS shorthand for the parent directory of a subdirectory. This attempt fails, however, because DOS regards H:\ as a root directory, which has no parent.

Root maps are handy for several things. They enable applications to work on networks even though they may insist on working with files in root or first-level directories. You can make a network directory look like a C: drive, which enables applications to network even though they will not work with drive letters above C:, D:, or E:. Root maps also reduce confusion by hiding directories that you needn't be aware of. Most users don't need to know that 100 user home directories exist, for example. It is probably a good idea to map their home directories as root drives.

Search maps give NetWare and applications the capability to execute command files that are not in the default directory.

NetWare uses search maps much as DOS uses the directory path, and Netware creates a search map by mapping a drive letter to a directory and then placing the drive letter in the DOS path. Search maps can be referred to by the drive letter; in addition, they are sometimes referenced by search drive numbers, which are represented by S1 through S16.

The DOS PATH

If DOS needs to find an executable file that is not in the current directory, it searches through directories listed in its path to locate the file. The path is a list of directories that is stored in a memory area called the *environment*. DOS sets aside a portion of available memory to store the definitions of several environment *variables*, which consist of names, each of which represents a series or "string" of characters. These names and strings have meanings to DOS, NetWare, and their applications.

The DOS path is an example of an environment variable. The path is usually defined by the DOS PATH command. Your AUTOEXEC.BAT file may contain a path like the following:

```
PATH C:\DOS;C:\WINDOWS;C:\123
```

This path contains references to three directories separated by semicolons. After a command is executed and the command file cannot be found in the present directory, DOS searches the directories in the path, working from the first directory to the last, in an attempt to find the command file.

You can view all of the DOS environment variables by typing the following command from the command line:

```
SET
```

DOS responds with the following message:

```
COMSPEC=C:\COMMAND.COM
PROMPT=$p$g
PATH=C:\DOS;C:\WINDOWS;C:\123
```

NetWare implements search drives by manipulating the DOS path. NetWare assigns a drive letter chosen from the last available letter at the end of the alphabet. Then the drive letter is inserted into the PATH variable. If search drives Z:, Y:, and X: have been defined, the PATH variable may look like this:

```
PATH=Z:.;Y:.;C:\DOS;C:\WINDOWS;C:\123;X:.
```

Notice that each search-drive entry is followed by a period. The period is DOS shorthand for "the current directory." Thus the path points to the current directory mapped to the specified drive letter, regardless of the specific directory name.

Files

Virtually everything that is stored permanently on a computer is stored in *files*. A file is a named unit of disk storage that serves the same purpose as a file folder in a file cabinet; that is, it stores a related set of data.

Computers use two main types of files:

- *Program files* usually have name extensions of EXE or COM. These files contain instructions that are carried out by the computer's processor. Often, they are associated with commands that are typed at the DOS prompt. EDIT.COM, for example, is a file editor that is started by typing the command EDIT at the DOS prompt. Some EXE and COM files are used only by other executable files, however, so you may need to have some of these files even though you may never call them yourself.

  Large programs often use auxiliary files to store portions of the program that are required only occasionally. The files associated with these auxiliary programs are often called *overlay files* because they may load on top of other programs. Overlay files may have an extension such as OVL.

- *Data files* comprise just about every other type of file. Data files can be simple text files, which you can create with a text editor and read directly. These files are often called *ASCII files* because they are stored by using a standard code, called ASCII, which represents characters with binary numbers. Other data files are created and used by programs, and may make no sense at all to you if you try to examine them. Some files, such as the NetWare bindery, may be deliberately scrambled to make interpretation difficult for any but the intended program.

Program and data files exhibit different behaviors. When you access a program file, for example, your computer usually calls the file, loads the program, and then releases the file. The file then becomes immediately available for other users. If you access a data file, however, you often want to reserve the file for your exclusive use to prevent others from modifying the word processing document or the database record that you are currently changing. NetWare enables you to place *locks* on files.

Although users frequently need to modify data files, they seldom need to change the contents of program files. Program files, therefore, are frequently marked so they cannot be changed.

When you work with program and data files, it is important to identify all files that are related. To move a program, you must also move any overlay or data files that it requires. When you work with data files, be aware that the data may be spread throughout several files; in addition, still more files may be required for the indexes to the files. Users must have appropriate access to all required program and data files for a given application by being able to find the files (are the files in the default directory or in search maps?) and by having appropriate access privileges to each file.

File and Directory Attributes

NetWare assigns *attributes* or *flags* to files and directories to signify the ways in which they can be manipulated. Some flags are altered by programs, others by users. An example is the Sharable flag, which enables data files to be accessed by multiple simultaneous users.

Table 1.1 summarizes the flags used by NetWare. Notice that some flags are specific to different versions of NetWare. Some flags can be applied to files or directories only.

Table 1.1
Netware Directory and File Attributes

Flag	Symbol	File	Directory	2.x	3.x
Archive	A	✓		✓	✓

Indicates that the file should be backed up. This flag is assigned by NetWare whenever a file is modified and is used by backup software to identify changed files.

Copy Inhibit	C	✓			✓

Prevents Macintosh users from copying the file, regardless of Read or File Scan rights. The user must have Modify rights to remove this flag.

Delete Inhibit	D	✓	✓		✓

Prevents users from deleting the flagged directory or file, regardless of Erase rights. Modify rights are required to remove this flag.

Execute Only	X	✓		✓	✓

Prevents EXE or COM files from being copied or backed up. This flag cannot be removed; the file must be deleted and restored from the program disks. Some programs are incompatible with Execute Only.

continues

Table 1.1
continued

Flag	Symbol	File	Directory	2.x	3.x
Hidden	H	✓	✓	✓	✓

Prevents files and directories from appearing in the DOS DIR command lists. They appear in NDIR listings if the user has File Scan rights.

Flag	Symbol	File	Directory	2.x	3.x
Indexed	I	3		3	✓

Instructs NetWare to maintain an index on the file, speeding access to large files. This flag has no effect in 3.x, which automatically indexes large files.

Flag	Symbol	File	Directory	2.x	3.x
Normal	N	✓	✓		

Indicates that no attributes have been assigned. Functions like the Public folder on a Macintosh.

Flag	Symbol	File	Directory	2.x	3.x
Private	P		✓	✓	

Prevents users from seeing this directory, but enables access to subdirectories. Corresponds to the Macintosh Private folder.

Flag	Symbol	File	Directory	2.x	3.x
Purge	P	✓	✓		✓

Indicates that the file or files in the directory should be purged immediately after deletion. Purged files cannot be recovered with SALVAGE.

Flag	Symbol	File	Directory	2.x	3.x
Read Only	Ro	✓		✓	✓

Prevents files from being modified, deleted, or renamed. This flag is especially appropriate for program files.

Flag	Symbol	File	Directory	2.x	3.x
Read Write	Rw	✓		✓	✓

Enables you to modify, delete, or rename files if the user has appropriate rights. Rw is the opposite of Ro, and the two are mutually exclusive.

Flag	Symbol	File	Directory	2.x	3.x
Rename Inhibit	R	✓	✓	✓	

Prevents renaming of files or directories. Users must have Modify rights to remove this flag.

Flag	Symbol	File	Directory	2.x	3.x
Shareable	S	✓		✓	✓

Permits more than one user to access the file simultaneously.

System	Sy	✓	✓	✓	✓

Identifies files or directories as system files or directories. The DOS DIR command cannot list system files or directories. NDIR lists them if the user has File Scan rights.

Transactional	T	✓		✓	✓

Indicates that the file is to be monitored by the Transactional Tracking System (TTS).

Tasks

Creating Volumes in NetWare 2.2

Purpose

In NetWare 2.2 the INSTALL utility is used to create NetWare volumes. This must be done while the server is down.

To add a volume to a Netware 2.2 partition, space must be taken from an existing volume. Follow the procedure described in Appendix A to reconfigure a NetWare 2.2 server. At step 5, use the following procedure to modify the volume information table:

Steps

1. Identify the disk number that will contain the new volume.

2. Identify a volume on that disk that can be reduced in size.

3. Reduce the Megabytes field value for that volume. INSTALL warns you that this procedure causes data loss.

4. Netware creates a new volume entry in the table containing the freed storage. You can modify the name.

5. Restore data as required from your tape backups.

Notes

Volumes on 2.x servers are rarely redefined after you create them. Changes must be made by using the NetWare INSTALL utility. Any change in size erases the files on the volume, so the files must be archived and restored after the volume is resized.

If you have only one physical drive, you can make the SYS: volume as large as the disk. Any space not allocated to SYS: is placed in volumes named VOL1, VOL2, and so forth. Additional volumes are created by INSTALL as you add new hard disks.

Creating Volumes in NetWare 3.11

Purpose

To add a new volume to a NetWare 3.x server, use the INSTALL NLM. NetWare 3.x uses the INSTALL NLM to create volumes while the server is up.

Steps

1. Start INSTALL from the system console by typing

    LOAD INSTALL

2. Select **System Options** from the INSTALL menu.

3. The **Volumes** window displays names of the existing volumes. Begin to add a new volume by pressing Ins. If no space is available, NetWare responds

```
There are no free areas available for a volume.
```

You cannot continue with this task.

4. If more than one partition has free space, NetWare displays a box with the list **Free Space Available for Volume Segments**. Select the segment that is to receive the new volume.

   The **New Volume Information** form is displayed. The cursor is in the **Volume Name** field.

5. Enter a name for the volume. If this is the first volume, it must be named SYS:; otherwise, it can be any name that is unique in the partition you selected.

6. Press Enter to move to the **Block Size** field.

7. Press Enter to display the Block Size menu. Select the desired block size and press Enter.

8. Select a block size.

9. Press the down-arrow key to move to the **Initial Segment Size** field.

10. Accept the number displayed to allocate all available blocks in the segment to this volume. Reduce this number if you want a smaller volume. For a given size in megabytes, calculate the number of blocks as follows:

    Divide 1024 by the block size to determine blocks per megabyte. For 4K blocks, for example, use the following formula:

    $1024 / 4 = 256$ blocks per megabyte

    Multiply blocks per megabyte by the desired volume size in megabytes. For a 30M volume with 4K blocks, the calculation is as follows:

    $256 \times 30 = 7680$ blocks

    Enter this number in the **Volume Size** field.

11. To create the volume, press Esc. Then select **Yes** from the menu. After the volume is created, press Enter to return to the **Volume Information** box.

12. Highlight the new volume and press Enter.

13. Highlight the **Status** field and press Enter.

14. Select **Mount Volume**.

Notes

Use the following guidelines to select block size:

- If in doubt, the default 4K block size is usually a good compromise.

- After a volume is created, its block size cannot be changed.

- Although small blocks use disk space more efficiently, they require more server memory. 2K blocks use twice the memory of 4K blocks.

- Large blocks use less server memory and are ideal if you use the volume primarily to store large database files. You may want to create a volume specifically for database files. For very large files, choose 32K or 64K blocks. (Some DOS utilities may report erroneous free space on volumes with 32K or 64K blocks.)

Enlarging Volumes in NetWare 2.2

Purpose

To add space to a volume in NetWare 2.x, you must reconfigure the file server. Because enlarging a volume deletes all data in the volume, always back up the volume before you reconfigure it, and then restore the files afterward.

Steps

1. To enlarge a volume in NetWare 2.2, follow the procedures described in the Appendix for reconfiguring the file server.

2. Make the desired volume changes in step 5. To add space to one volume, you must take space from another because INSTALL assigns all available space to volumes. You can reserve space in an unused volume for future allocation to other volumes.

Enlarging Volumes in NetWare 3.11

Purpose

NetWare 3.x has a significant advantage of enabling you to add disk segments to volumes without having to reinstall or losing data. This task teaches you how to enlarge an existing volume on a NetWare 3.x server.

Steps

1. Start INSTALL from the system console by typing

   LOAD INSTALL

2. Select **System Options** from the INSTALL menu.

3. Select the desired volume from the **Volumes** list.

4. Move to the **Volume Segments** field and press Enter. A list of the segments currently in the volume is displayed.

5. Press Ins.

   If NetWare displays the message

   `There are no free areas available for a volume.`

   you cannot continue with this task.

6. If more than one disk segment is available, a list is displayed. Select the desired segment.

7. Enter the number of blocks to be added to the volume and press Enter.

8. Select **Yes** to add the segment to the volume.

Notes

If unallocated disk space is available on a NetWare 3.11 volume, you easily can expand the volume's capacity. To reduce a volume's size, however, the volume must be deleted and re-created. All data must be backed up before the volume is resized and then restored afterward.

Managers of Netware 3.x servers may want to reserve some partition space so that space can be added to volumes as storage requirements increase. Netware 3.x accommodates volumes that span multiple hard disks, but Novell recommends this practice only if all disks are mirrored.

Creating Directories with the MD Command

Purpose

The DOS MD (Make Directory) command and the FILER utility enable you to create directories. Most volumes are divided into directories and subdirectories.

Steps

1. To create the directory HOME at the root of the current volume, type

   `MD \HOME`

2. You must create subdirectories a level at a time. If `\HOME` exists, create the directory DSMITH as a subdirectory of `\HOME`, by typing

   `MD \HOME\DSMITH`

3. You now can create a worksheet directory. Use this command:

   `MD \HOME\DSMITH\WKSHEETS`

4. If `\HOME` is your current directory, the following shortcuts are available:

MD DSMITH

or

MD .\DSMITH

In the first example, the directory is created as a subdirectory of the current directory because the command omits the \ before **HOME**. The second example uses a period (.) to denote the current directory. If a period is used, a \ must precede **HOME**.

Don't try to create a subdirectory of HOME by using the command **MD \DSMITH** because this command places DSMITH as a directory at the root of the current volume, not under HOME.

To create a directory on a volume other than the current one, you can include the volume name. Use the following command format:

MD DATA:HOME

Creating Directories from **FILER**

Purpose

You also can use the NetWare FILER to create directories. The following example assumes that the current directory will not contain the new subdirectory.

Steps

1. Run FILER.

2. From FILER's **Available Topics** menu, choose **Select Current Directory**.

    FILER displays the current directory.

3. You can edit the directory information and press Enter, or select from menus by performing the following actions:

- Backspace over the complete directory path.

- Press Ins.

- Select the server name. The server name is stored in the path display.

- Select the volume name. The volume name is added to the path.

- Select successive directory names until you build the path that you want.

- Press Esc to return the main FILER menu.

4. Select **Directory Contents**.

   FILER displays a list of files and subdirectories in the current directory.

5. Press Ins.

6. Enter the name of the new subdirectory.

   After you press Enter, the directory contents are redisplayed, including the new directory.

Deleting Directories

Purpose

Use the FILER utility to delete entire directory structures in one operation.

Steps

1. Run FILER.

2. From FILER's Available Topics menu, choose **Select Current Directory**.

3. Enter the directory path that contains the directory that you want to delete. Use the method described in the "Creating Directories" task to select the directory path from menus.

4. Return to the FILER menu and select **Display Directory Contents**.

5. Highlight the directory you want to delete.

6. Press Del.

7. You can elect to delete files only or to delete the entire directory structure.

Notes

Deleting directories with FILER is easier than using DOS commands. In DOS, files must be removed from each level of the directory structure and each subdirectory level must be deleted one at a time.

Mapping Directories to Drives

Purpose

Drive mapping enables users and programs to refer to complete NetWare directory structures by a single drive letter. These drive maps behave much like A:, B:, C:, and other DOS volumes that are associated with the user's workstation.

NetWare drive maps use letters starting from F: and work toward the end of the alphabet. Search drives start lettering from Z: and work toward the beginning of the alphabet. Ordinarily, you will want to choose your drive map letters from the range of F: through Q:.

Steps

The most basic form of a MAP command is similar to this:

```
MAP M:=SYS:APPS\EDIT
```

After executing this command, typing

```
M:
```

changes you to the SYS:APPS\EDIT directory. If your prompt displays the current directory path, it looks something like this:

```
M:\APPS\EDIT>
```

You almost always have several drive mappings in effect.
To display these mappings, type

MAP

The resulting display resembles this:

```
Drive  A:   maps to a local disk.
Drive  B:   maps to a local disk.
Drive  C:   maps to a local disk.
Drive  D:   maps to a local disk.
Drive  E:   maps to a local disk.
Drive  F: = FS1\SYS:  \LOGIN
Drive  M: = FS1\SYS:  \APPS\EDIT
     — —
SEARCH1:  = Z:. [FS1\SYS:  \PUBLIC]
SEARCH2:  = C:\DOS
```

Drives A: through E: remain mapped to disks on the
workstation. DOS usually reserves those five drive letters
for itself. You can modify this default by adding a LASTDRIVE
command to the PC's CONFIG.SYS file. If CONFIG.SYS contains
the following line:

```
LASTDRIVE=C
```

then NetWare starts mapping drives starting with D:,
which maps to the SYS:LOGIN directory. Although the
LASTDRIVE=C line makes two more drives readily available
to NetWare, it can cause confusion because NetWare maps
the LOGIN directory to F:. In general, it is preferable to have
all workstations on the LAN configured for the same basic
drive map letters.

After you establish a drive map, you can alter it with the CD
command. The following lines illustrate the current
directory path (the DOS prompt is included):

```
F:\LOGIN> MAP H:=SYS:HOME\DSMITH
F:\LOGIN> H:
H:\HOME\DSMITH> CD SPSHEET
H:\HOME\DSMITH\SPSHEET>
```

A list produced by the MAP command would include the
following about the H: drive:

```
Drive  H: = FS1\SYS:  \HOME\DSMITH\SPSHEET
```

The CD command has remapped drive H: to the SPSHEET subdirectory. Similarly, the following lines demonstrate that drive H: can be mapped to the HOME directory:

```
H:\HOME\DSMITH\SPSHEET> CD ..
H:\HOME\DSMITH> CD ..
H:\HOME>
```

You may not want drive maps to behave in this manner. The system administrator, for example, may want to prevent users from changing to the HOME directory from their personal home directory. In addition, some applications require that certain files be in the root directory. MAP can map subdirectories so that they appear to be at the root of a volume. The following example illustrates this technique:

```
F:\LOGIN> MAP ROOT H:=SYS:HOME\DSMITH
F:\LOGIN> H:
H:>
```

The preceding H: prompt demonstrates that DOS thinks it is working with a root-level directory. A MAP list would now display the H: drive like this:

```
Drive  H: = FS1\SYS:HOME\DSMITH  \
```

By placing the directory information to the left of the backslash (\), MAP informs you that this drive is mapped with the ROOT option.

To delete a drive map, use MAP DEL as in this example:

```
MAP DEL H:
```

Note that you cannot delete your default drive. If H: is your default, use the CD command to switch to another drive before trying to delete H:.

Mapping Search Drives

Purpose

Search drives are the preferred way of working with the search path in NetWare. Users create network search drives by number, from S1 through S16. MAP assigns drive letters to search drives starting with the last available letter in the alphabet.

Steps

To map the first search drive to the server's PUBLIC directory, type

MAP S1:=SYS:PUBLIC

A MAP list may report this drive as

```
SEARCH1:  = Z:. [FS1\SYS:  \PUBLIC]
```

If a map to S1: exists before the preceding command is entered, the existing map is overwritten.

To add a search drive to the last search position, try to map it as S16:. MAP moves it to the last available slot. Consider this example:

MAP S16:=SYS:APPS\EDIT

If several other search drives existed previously, a MAP listing may look like this:

```
Drive  A:   maps to a local disk.
Drive  B:   maps to a local disk.
Drive  C:   maps to a local disk.
Drive  D:   maps to a local disk.
Drive  E:   maps to a local disk.
Drive  F: = FS1\SYS:  \LOGIN
Drive  M: = FS1\SYS:  \APPS\EDIT
  __  __
SEARCH1:  = Z:. [FS1\SYS:  \PUBLIC]
SEARCH2:  = C:\DOS
SEARCH3:  = Y:. [FS1\SYS:  \UTILITIES
SEARCH4:  = C:\WINDOWS
SEARCH5:  = X:  [FS1\SYS:  \APPS\EDIT
```

Even though the MAP command specified S16: the search drive was mapped to S5:, which was the next available slot.

The MAP INSERT: command enables you to define a search drive into a specific position, as in the following example:

MAP INSERT S1:=SYS:APPS\SPRDSHT

The search drives from the preceding example would now be remapped as follows:

```
SEARCH1:..= W:. [FS1\SYS:  \APPS\SPRDSHT
SEARCH2:  = Z:. [FS1\SYS:  \PUBLIC]
```

```
SEARCH3:   = C:\DOS
SEARCH4:   = Y:. [FS1\SYS:   \UTILITIES
SEARCH5:   = C:\WINDOWS
SEARCH6:   = X:. [FS1\SYS:   \APPS\EDIT
```

Although the previous search drives were renumbered, they retained their original drive letters. The new search drive is assigned to W:, which is the next available letter. Search drives can be inserted anywhere in the search drive list with the INSERT option.

The best way to delete a search drive is to delete it by its drive number as follows:

MAP DEL S1:

You can change your default directory to a search directory by changing to the drive letter. Use caution when you use CD. The drive is mapped to a new directory and a needed search drive may be lost. In the following sample lines, the search map to SYS:PUBLIC is lost, and the PUBLIC utilities are no longer available:

```
F:\LOGIN>Z:
Z:\PUBLIC>WHOAMI
You are user DSMITH attached to server FS1,
connection 1.
Server FS1 is running Dedicated NetWare V2.2(50)
Rev. A.
Login time: Thursday  December  5, 1991  12:27 am

Z:\PUBLIC>CD ..
Z:\>WHOAMI

Bad command or file name
```

A better technique is to map a standard drive to the desired directory and to use that drive instead of the search drive letter.

Accessing Files on Other Servers

Purpose

If several servers are available, users frequently need to access applications of different servers in quick succession.

Rather than forcing them to log out of each server prior to logging into another, NetWare permits users to connect to a total of eight servers simultaneously.

Steps

To attach to a server, you must have an account on that server. If you are logged in on server FS1, you can attach to FS2 using the following commands:

```
F:\LOGIN>ATTACH FS2
Username: DSMITH
Password:
```

Note that the password does not appear on the screen.

Attaching is most convenient if your login IDs and passwords are the same on all servers. Usually the SETPASS command synchronizes your password for all attached servers when you change it.

You may not need to explicitly attach to a server before you request a service from it. If you attempt to map a drive to an unattached server, NetWare asks you for the server account information, as in this example:

```
MAP Q:=FS1/SYS:LOGIN
```

After you press Enter, the screen displays the following prompts:

```
Enter user name for server FS1: DSMITH
Enter your password for server FS1:
Your station is attached to server FS1.
Drive  Q: = FS2\SYS:  \LOGIN
```

After you finish using services on **FS2**, you can detach from it. Log off of that specific server by using this command:

```
LOGOUT FS2
```

Setting File Attributes with FLAG

Purpose

File attributes can be set and changed from the command line or from within FILER. Both methods are discussed in this section because each method has its advantages. Before you begin, review the discussion about file attributes in the Concepts section of this chapter for more information. The user must have Modify rights (see Chapter 3) to change a file's attributes.

Steps

The FLAG command accepts a path specification to define the files and directories to be modified. Several possible path specifications are explained in the following discussions.

To view the attributes of all files in SYS:APPS\EDIT, type

    FLAG SYS:APPS\EDIT

All files in the directory are listed along with their current attributes. If drive M: is mapped to SYS:APPS\EDIT, you can view the attributes of all files by entering

    FLAG M:

If your current directory is SYS:APPS\EDIT, just type

    FLAG

To display the attributes of a specific group of files in the current directory, type

    FLAG *.EXE RO S

If M: is mapped to SYS:APPS\EDIT, mark all files in that directory Shareable Read Only by typing

    FLAG M: S RO

To flag the .DAT database files in the current directory as Transactional and as Delete Inhibit, type

    FLAG *.DAT T D

To remove the T attribute from the same files, type

    FLAG *.DAT -T

FLAG accepts + and - to add or remove flags respectively. The attributes to be added and removed should be grouped after the appropriate sign. To add T and D and remove H and P, type

```
FLAG * +T D -H P
```

You may discover that -RW is the same as RO and that -RO is the same as RW. RO and RW are mutually exclusive.

To clear all attributes for a set of COM files, include NORMAL in the flag position, as in the following example:

```
FLAG F:\APPS\UTILITY\*.COM NORMAL
```

To set all available flags for a file, type the following command:

```
FLAG F:\HOME\DSMITH\MYDOC.DOC ALL
```

Changing Directory Attributes with FLAGDIR

Purpose

FLAGDIR works with directories much as FLAG works with files. You can view the attributes of the current directory by using the FLAGDIR command.

Steps

To view the attributes of the current directory, simply type

```
FLAGDIR
```

To view attributes of the subdirectories under the current directory, enter

```
FLAGDIR *
```

To view the attributes of any directory, include the directory path. The following command displays the attributes of all root-level directories:

```
FLAGDIR SYS:*
```

Directory attributes can exist at the root of a volume. To view these attributes, type

```
FLAGDIR SYS:
```

To flag the current directory with the purge attribute, remember that a period represents the current directory.

Type the following command:

FLAGDIR . P

Using **FILER** to Change File and Directory Attributes

Purpose

The FILER utility makes it easy for you to modify file and directory attributes with a point-and-shoot method. You do not need to remember all of the possible attribute combinations because FILER uses menus to list all available attributes. FILER can flag files or directories only one at a time, so you should remain familiar with FLAG and FLAGDIR so that you can work with large groups of files.

Steps

To modify the attributes for a file using FILER, follow these steps:

1. Start FILER.

2. If desired, use the **Select Current Directory** option to change directories.

3. Select **Display Directory Contents**.

4. Highlight the file to be modified and press Enter.

5. Select **View/Set File Information**. The abbreviated attributes for the file appear in the field that is highlighted on the next screen.

6. Press Enter to display the **Current File Attributes** box.

7. For each attribute that you want to remove, highlight the attribute and press Del.

8. To add attributes, press Ins to display the **Other File Attributes** box.

9. Highlight the first desired attribute. If that is the only new attribute, press Enter.

10. To select additional attributes, press F5. The current attribute is displayed in a new color (usually yellow on a color monitor) to indicate that it has been selected. Select more attributes by highlighting them and pressing F5. After you select all attributes, press Enter.

The attribute changes appear in the abbreviated **File Attributes** display.

To modify the attributes for a directory using FILER, follow these steps:

1. Start FILER.

2. If desired, use the **Select Current Directory** option to change directories.

3. Select **Display Directory Contents**.

4. Highlight the directory you want to modify and press Enter.

5. Select **View/Set Directory Information**.

6. Highlight the message see list following **Directory Attributes** and press Enter to display the **Current Attributes** box.

7. For each attribute that you want to remove, highlight the attribute and press Del.

8. To add attributes press Ins to display the **Other Attributes** box.

9. Highlight the first attribute you want to add. If that is the only new attribute, press Enter.

10. To select additional attributes, press F5. The current attribute is displayed in a new color (usually yellow on a color monitor) to indicate that it has been selected. Select more attributes by highlighting them and pressing F5. After you select all attributes, press Enter.

The attribute changes appear in the abbreviated File Attributes display.

Changing File and Directory Ownership

Purpose

Use the FILER utility to change the ownership of files and directories. File and directory ownership help track users' disk utilization. The NetWare ownership information often does not correspond to what is desired. For example, if SUPERVISOR creates a user's home directory and copies files into that directory, the directory and all files are owned by SUPERVISOR and do not count against the user's storage allocation. FILER can change the ownership as required.

Steps

You usually alter ownership at the directory level, which is illustrated in the following steps:

1. Start FILER.

2. If necessary change directories using **Select Current Directory**.

3. Select **Current Directory Information**.

   The **Directory Information** box is displayed with the highlight on the current directory owner.

4. Press Enter to display a list of user IDs.

5. Select the ID of the user that you want to make the owner of the directory, and then press Enter. The selected ID appears in the **Owner** field.

Performing File Listings with NDIR

Purpose

Use NDIR to sort files and specify files and subdirectories with virtually any characteristic. NDIR is a powerful directory listing tool that can be used much like the DOS DIR command. Unlike the DIR command, however, NDIR lists hidden or system files and directories.

Steps

To perform standard listings, use NDIR without any options. For example, type the command

NDIR SYS:PUBLIC*.EXE

This command produces the following output:

```
FS2/SYS:PUBLIC

Files:          Size    Last Updated      Flags
Owner
 _  _  _  _    _  _  _   _  _  _  _  _  _   _  _  _  _  _  _  _  _  _   _  _
13T020    EXE   77,071   8-14-90   0:00   [RoS— — — — — —DR]  FS2
20UPDATE  EXE   41,045   8-14-90   0:00   [RoS— — — — — —DR]  FS2
ALLOW     EXE   21,049   1-29-91   8:56a  [RoS— — — — — —DR]  FS2
ATTACH    EXE   35,169   1-23-91  10:44a  [RoS— — — — — —DR]  FS2
BCONSOLE  EXE   48,686   2-01-91  10:09a  [RoS— — — — — —DR]  FS2
BREQUEST  EXE   18,060   2-12-91   5:25p  [RoS— — — — — —DR]  FS2
BROLLFWD  EXE   31,438   2-20-91   1:54p  [RoS— — — — — —DR]  FS2
CAPTURE   EXE   49,505   1-28-91   4:21p  [RoS— — — — — —DR]  FS2
CASTOFF   EXE   12,023   1-22-91  10:12a  [RoS— — — — — —DR]  FS2
CASTON    EXE    8,215   1-22-91  10:12a  [RoS— — — — — —DR]  FS2
CHKDIR    EXE   19,013   1-25-91   3:53p  [RoS— — — — — —DR]  FS2
CHKVOL    EXE   33,127   1-26-91   7:19a  [RoS— — — — — —DR]  FS2
COLORPAL  EXE   50,176  10-20-87   9:33a  [RoS— — — — — —DR]  FS2
DSPACE    EXE  136,775   1-29-91   3:50p  [RoS— — — — — —DR]  FS2
ENDCAP    EXE   13,553   7-19-89  10:55a  [RoS— — — — — —DR]  FS2
FCONSOLE  EXE  208,866   2-08-91  12:01p  [RoS— — — — — —DR]  FS2
FILER     EXE  292,951   2-01-91   8:31a  [RoS— — — — — —DR]  FS2
FLAG      EXE   43,409   1-30-91   4:56p  [RoS— — — — — —DR]  FS2
FLAGDIR   EXE   32,309   2-01-91   4:34p  [RoS— — — — — —DR]  FS2
```

```
Strike any key for next page or C for continuous display...
```

After the remainder of this list appears, a summary is displayed much like the following:

```
4,752,530 bytes in   65 files
4,874,240 bytes in 1190 blocks
```

If you are a system manager, you may need a list of all files owned by a particular individual. The NDIR command can provide this capability using search options and subdirectory searches. If you want to delete the user DSMITH and all files owned by that ID, for example, the following NDIR command lists all of the target files:

NDIR SYS:* /OWNER EQUAL DSMITH SUB

The report from such a command can be large and can take several minutes to generate.

In this example, two options follow the backslash. Only one backslash (/) is required. It should appear before the first option. The options can appear in any order.

The first option is OWNER EQUAL, which should be followed by a user login ID. The second option is SUB, which instructs NDIR to search all subdirectories of the specified directory. All files on the volume are listed in this example because this command starts at the root of the SYS: volume.

Another useful option identifies files that have not been accessed since a specified date. This option can help you identify old, dormant data files that can be deleted when your server runs short of disk storage space.

```
NDIR SYS:HOME\DSMITH\*.* /ACCESS NOT AFTER 5-31-91 SUB
```

The preceding example uses NOT to invert the operation of the ACCESS AFTER option. The ACCESS AFTER option uses NetWare's Last Accessed date stamp for the files. Unfortunately, some tape backup software resets the Last Accessed date to the current date every time the file is archived. If your software does this, you can get an idea of the number of dormant files with the following format:

```
NDIR SYS:HOME\DSMITH\*.* /UPDATE NOT AFTER 5-31-91 SUB
```

The preceding command lists only files that have not been modified since the specified date.

NDIR also has options to control the ways in which files and directories are sorted. To sort files by creation date, follow the format in this example:

```
NDIR SYS:HOME\DSMITH\*.* /REV SORT CREATE
```

The REV switch reverses the normal sorting order so that files are listed starting with the most recently created ones.

Notes

NDIR has many options that you can use to modify the data displayed in the report columns. These options are listed in Table 1.2. For consistency, the options are presented using the same conventions Novell uses in NetWare documentation. Please use the following rules as you interpret the structure of the options:

- Items that appear in square brackets ([and]) are optional.

- You can abbreviate some options; the abbreviation appears in uppercase letters within the full command.

- Some options may accept one of several mutually exclusive choices. The choices are separated by a vertical bar (|). In all cases, one of the options must be chosen.

- Dates are signified as *mm-dd-yy*. As you enter the commands, all three sections must be completed with a number. Leading zeros are not required. Years can be entered as two or four digits.

Table 1.2
Options for the NDIR Utility

[NOT] A	Lists files flagged Archive needed
[NOT] EX	Lists files flagged Execute Only
[NOT] H	Lists files flagged Hidden
[NOT] I	Lists files flagged Indexed
[NOT] RO	Lists files flagged Read Only
[NOT] S	Lists files flagged Shareable
[NOT] SY	Lists files flagged System
[NOT] T	Lists files flagged Transactional
ACCESS [NOT] BEFore¦EQual¦ before AFTer *mm-dd-yy*	Lists files last accessed on, or after the date specified
ARCHIVE [NOT} BEFore¦ EQual¦AFTer *mm-dd-yy*	Lists files archived before, or after the date specified.
CReate [NOT} BEFore¦EQual¦ ¦AFTer *mm-dd-yy*	Lists files created before, on, or after the date specified.

DATES	Displays time and date information for the files, including dates last archived, accessed, or modified, as well as the creation date.
[REVerse] SORT ACcess	Lists files by last access date from earliest to latest.
[REVerse] SORT ARchive	Lists files by last archive date from earliest to latest.
[REVerse] SORT CReate	Lists files by creation date from earliest to latest.
[REVerse] SORT UPdate	Lists files by date of last change from earliest to latest.
[REVerse] SORT OWner	Lists files by owner in alphabetical order.
[REVerse] SORT SIze	Lists files by size, from smallest to largest.
[REVerse] SORT UNsorted	Lists files unsorted.
UPdate [NOT] BEFore¦ EQual¦AFTer mm-dd-yy	Lists files last changed before, on, or after the date specified.
DO	Lists subdirectory information only.
SUB	Lists information for all subdirectories under the primary directory
FO	Lists directory files only.
MAC	Lists Macintosh files and subdirectories
OWner [NOT] name	Lists files owned by user specified by name.
RIGHTS	Displays your maximum and effective rights in subdirectories.
SIze [NOT] GR¦EQ¦LE nnn	Lists files having a size GReater than, EQual to, or LEss than nnn.

Copying Files with COPY, XCOPY, and NCOPY

Purpose

This task familiarizes you with the NetWare NCOPY command.

Steps

You can copy NetWare files by using the DOS COPY or XCOPY command as well as the NetWare NCOPY command. COPY and XCOPY are limited, however, when you work on a network because they are not NetWare commands.

Copying NetWare Files with COPY

COPY has two deficiencies:

- COPY does not understand directory paths that include server or volume names.

- COPY cannot copy NetWare file attributes.

If directory paths can be expressed by drive letters or by directory paths on the current volume, COPY can duplicate files. You can copy files using the following command examples, which assume that F: is properly mapped to a NetWare volume:

```
COPY F:\HOME\DSMITH\*.* C:\MYHOME
COPY *.* \APPS\EDIT
```

The COPY command cannot be used in the following examples:

```
COPY SYS:APPS\EDIT C:\EDIT
COPY PS1/APPS:HOME\DSMITH C:\MYHOME
```

If you try to use this format, the error message Too many parameters appears.

Copying NetWare Files with XCOPY

The XCOPY command is trickier than the COPY command. COPY simply stops with an error when it is asked to work with a NetWare volume identifier. XCOPY acts on the command, but it may do the wrong thing.

If the referenced drive letters are properly mapped, the following XCOPY operations will work (recall that /S instructs XCOPY to copy subdirectories as well as the primary directory):

```
XCOPY F:\HOME\DSMITH C:\MYHOME /S
XCOPY F:*.* F:\TEMP /S
```

If a \TEMP directory exists on the SYS: volume, XCOPY also performs the following operation correctly:

```
XCOPY *.* SYS:TEMP
```

If SYS:TEMP has not been created, however, XCOPY goes awry. Instead of creating a \TEMP directory at the root of SYS:, XCOPY creates a SYS subdirectory of the current directory and then copies the source files into the new subdirectory.

When using XCOPY on NetWare volumes, always reference drive map letters. Server and volume names in the directory paths can spell trouble.

Copying NetWare Files with NCOPY

Use NCOPY when you work with NetWare volumes. It offers more options than COPY or XCOPY, and NCOPY duplicates all NetWare file attributes with the files. In addition, NCOPY uses network resources more efficiently.

Consider the following COPY command:

```
COPY F:\HOME\DSMITH\*.* F:\TEMP
```

Executing COPY starts a program running in your local PC. To copy files between the two NetWare directories, the contents of the files are first copied from the server source directory to the PC's memory; then they are copied from the PC memory to the destination directory. All of the file information must, therefore, be transferred through the network twice, both to and from your PC.

NCOPY works in cooperation with the server. When transferring files between NetWare volumes, the file data is not copied through the network. Instead, the server performs the copy itself. Network traffic is considerably reduced. NCOPY should always be used for copying files between NetWare volumes.

The way in which NCOPY works is similar to XCOPY. Consider the following example:

NCOPY \APPS\EDIT*.EXE G:\UTILITY\EDIT /S
NCOPY C:\TEMP F:\HOME\DSMITH /S

Unlike XCOPY, however, NCOPY understands NetWare directory paths, and it is possible to copy without drive letters. NCOPY can even copy between two servers if the user is attached to both servers, as in this example:

NCOPY FS1/SYS:APPS\SPSHEET FS2\APPS:SPSHEET /S

Note that NCOPY does not operate properly when forward slashes are used as directory separators. The following sample command illustrates this limitation:

```
F:\>NCOPY /HOME/DSMITH /TEMP
An unknown switch (OME/DSMITH) was found on the command line.
An unknown switch (DSMITH) was found on the command line.
An unknown switch (TH) was found on the command line.
An unknown switch (TEMP) was found on the command line.
Usage:  NCOPY [path] [[TO] path] [option]
Options /s      copy subdirectories.
        /s/e    copy subdirectories, including empty directories.
        /f      copy sparse files.
        /i      inform when non-DOS file information will be lost.
        /c      copy only DOS information.
        /a      copy files with archive bit set.
        /m      copy files with archive bit set, clear the bit.
        /v      verify with a read after every write.
        /h (/?) display this usage message.
F:\>
```

Instead of identifying /HOME/DSMITH as the source directory, NCOPY thought the slash identified an option. You can avoid this error in two ways. Either of the following commands performs the file copy correctly:

NCOPY \HOME\DSMITH \TEMP
NCOPY F:/HOME/DSMITH F:/TEMP

Use backslashes to avoid this error in all circumstances.

Limiting Directory Size in NetWare 3.11

Purpose

The NetWare 3.x DSPACE utility enables you to limit the size of a directory. System managers may find it advantageous to limit the size of a directory. A department may be allocated 100 megabytes of storage for a database application.

Steps

DSPACE is a NetWare menu utility. To limit the size of the SYS:HOME\DSMITH directory to 1 megabyte, do the following:

1. Start DSPACE.

2. Select **Directory Restrictions**.

3. Edit the directory path to read PS1/SYS:HOME\DSMITH and press Enter.

4. Highlight the **Limit Space** field and enter Y.

5. Highlight the **Directory Space Limit** field and enter 1024.

6. Press Esc.

Note

Setting a space limit does not mean that the space is reserved for this directory. Users of this directory are still contending for the total space on the volume; if the volume fills up the directory can get no fuller even though it may be smaller than its maximum allotment.

Monitoring Volume File Usage

Purpose

Use the VOLINFO command to check each volume on a network. The system supervisor should check all volumes daily to ensure that they are not filling to near capacity.

Step

Type **VOLINFO** and press Enter.

Notes

The VOLINFO screen tracks volume storage dynamically. You can switch servers using the menu options provided.

Managing File Growth

Policing file use is one of the most nagging tasks a system administrator must face. It is an unfortunate fact that user storage requirements virtually always grow to exceed the space available. Users who no longer are bound by the fixed limit of a personal hard drive are often less careful with clearing out their directories. The tools presented in this section help you deal with storage crunches.

FILER enables you to ensure that file ownership is set properly so that you can hold users accountable for their storage use.

With NDIR, you can identify dormant or old files. Old files can be safely moved off to long-term tape storage. NDIR also enables you to identify such potential disk wasters as old backup (.BAK) files or temporary files that were created by applications but were not deleted due to a program malfunction.

DCONFIG allows for considerable flexibility in limiting department and user storage to manageable levels.

2

SECURITY

The value of the data on a network becomes apparent when the cost is considered if files are lost, damaged, or misappropriated. Ideally, you should prevent such loss by placing strong security restrictions on the network. The network has little use, however, if users cannot access the data they require. Openings in security must be provided. Network security management is always a balancing act between locking and unlocking system resources.

NetWare supplies tools that can assist the system administrator in successfully maintaining the required balance.

In this chapter you learn the following concepts:

- How to create and maintain user accounts

- How to ensure network security by using user account restrictions

- How to create groups and simplify the assignment of rights to large numbers of users

- How to give users and groups access to network services by granting them trustee assignments

- How rights are inherited by subdirectories and how rights masks can control which rights are inherited

- How to use the Read Only file attribute to enhance security

- How to maintain the NetWare bindery

Key Concepts

Before examining the commands and procedures presented in this chapter, you must have an understanding of the following terms:

- Users and groups
- User and group trustee assignments
- Inherited rights
- Read only and read write files

The following sections discuss these topics so that you have an understanding of the concept of granting specific rights to the users on your network.

Users and Groups

The starting point for NetWare security is the user *login name*. Each person who accesses the network is assigned a unique name, and the system administrator associates certain privileges and limitations to that name.

The user name is secured by a *password*, which the user must enter to gain access to the server. Users should be obligated to maintain secrecy of their password and to change the password periodically.

Users must be given specific access privileges to files on the server. Many networks have hundreds of users, and it would be a major task to assign all access privileges to users individually. NetWare supports the use of *groups*. Privileges can be assigned to groups, and users placed in those groups inherit the group privileges. If a change is made to a group's rights, all group members automatically are affected by the change. Proper use of groups is essential to the efficient management of a NetWare server.

NetWare creates and maintains a group named EVERYONE to which all users are automatically given membership. This group is used to confer privileges that are universal, such as the right to execute NetWare utilities that are installed in SYS:PUBLIC.

User and Group Trustee Assignments

NetWare confers user and group privileges by means of *trustee assignments*, which define the *rights* that a user or group has with regard to a server directory or file. A user can have rights to read the data in a file, for example, but not to modify the file's contents.

2.2	In common with all 2.x versions of NetWare, Version 2.2 can assign rights only to directories. All files in each directory are equally affected.

To make NetWare Version 2.2 similar to Version 3.11, Version 2.2 diverged from the rights definitions used in earlier revisions of NetWare. Users familiar with earlier versions of NetWare 2.x should review these new rights definitions carefully.

3.11	In addition to directory trustee assignments, NetWare Version 3.11 enables you to assign rights for specific files. File rights override directory rights. A user can have one set of trustee assignments that apply generally to all files in a directory, but can override the directory rights with individual rights for specific files.

Table 2.1 summarizes the directory rights that are common to both versions of NetWare. Table 2.2 describes additional rights that are unique to Version 3.x. Each right can be identified by a single letter, which is the first character of the right's name. You often see lists of rights identified by

these key letters and grouped in square brackets, for example [R C E F].

Table 2.1
Netware 2.2 and 3.11 Directory Rights

Right	Description
Access control	Grants the right to modify file or directory trustee assignments and the directory Inherited Rights Mask. Users having this right can grant rights that they themselves have not been given.
Create	Grants the right to create new files in the directory either with a program or by copying files into the directory. Users cannot access files they have created, however, unless they have Read or Write privileges for the directory. This feature is frequently used with electronic mail. A user can put a message into another's mail directory, but cannot view, modify, or delete files in that directory.
Erase	Grants the right to delete files, subdirectories, or the directory itself.
File scan	Grants the right to see files in the directory. Without this right, a user sees only an empty directory.
Modify	Grants the right to alter directory and file attributes, to rename directories, subdirectories, and files in the directory. In order to modify the contents of a file, the user must have the Write right.
Read	Grants the right to open files and examine the file's contents. This right is required to permit users to run programs stored in the directory.
Write	Grants the right to open and modify the contents of files.

Table 2.2
Additional Netware 3.11 Rights

Right	Description
Access control	Grants the right to modify trustee assignments and the Inherited Rights Mask for the file. Users having this right can grant rights that they themselves have not been given. Users cannot grant the Supervisory right, however.
Create	Grants the right to salvage a file after it has been deleted.
Erase	Grants the right to delete the file.
File scan	Grants the right to see the file in a directory listing.
Modify	Grants the right to alter file attributes and to rename the file. To modify the contents of a file, the user must have the Write right.
Read	Grants the right to open the file and examine its contents.
Supervisory	Grants all rights to the directory, its files, and its subdirectories. Also grants all rights to individual files. Supervisory rights circumvent all restrictions, including the Inherited Rights Masks. Users having this right can grant Supervisory rights to users or groups. The Supervisory right can only be revoked from the directory to which it was granted, not from files or subdirectories.
Write	Grants the right to open the file and modify its contents.

Inherited Rights

From the perspective of the subdirectory, the user inherits the rights that applied to that user in the parent directory unless something is done to prevent it. Rights assigned in a directory ordinarily apply to all subdirectories of that directory.

Consider a typical home directory structure. DSMITH's home directory may be SYS:HOME\DSMITH, a directory in which he has been granted R, W, E, C, M, F, and A rights. These rights also are available to DSMITH in SYS:HOME\DSMITH\SPRDSHT and SYS:HOME\DSMITH\DOCS by inheritance.

You can revoke rights from a group or user in a subdirectory by explicitly granting a smaller set of rights in that subdirectory.

2.2 Netware 2.2 assigns a *Maximum Rights Mask (MRM)* to each directory. The MRM sets an absolute limit to the rights users can have in a given directory. When a directory is created, the MRM is set to allow all rights, but rights can be reduced or eliminated altogether by restricting rights in the MRM. The MRM does not confer rights; it only controls which rights a directory can inherit. All users are affected by the MRM regardless of group or individual trustee assignments.

The MRM does not restrict the inheritance of rights. Restricting the MRM in a directory limits rights only in that directory, not in any subdirectories of that directory. The following example illustrates this situation:

SYS:ACCT	MRM	[	]
	Granted to Group ACCT	[R W C E M F]
	ACCT Effective Rights	

SYS:ACCT\BUDGET	MRM	[R F]
	ACCT Effective Rights	[R F]
SYS:ACCT\BUDGET\OLD	MRM	[R W C E M F A]
	ACCT Effective Rights	[R W C E M F]

Group ACCT was granted [R W C E M F A] rights in SYS:ACCT. The MRM masks all rights; however, and group ACCT has no effective rights in SYS:ACCT. The MRM was set to allow only R and F rights in SYS:ACCT\BUDGET. The effective rights of group ACCT in the BUDGET subdirectory, therefore, are only R and F. In the OLD subdirectory, however, rights are again set to [R W C E M F A]. The MRM in BUDGET had no effect on OLD, and all rights assigned in SYS.ACCT are inherited in the OLD subdirectory.

If you want to restrict the rights in the BUDGET and OLD directories, explicitly assign only the R and F rights to Group ACCT in the BUDGET subdirectory. This action revokes all other rights in BUDGET leaving only the R and F rights to be inherited by OLD.

SYS:ACCT	MRM	[ ]
	Granted to Group ACCT	[R W C E M F]
	ACCT Effective Rights	
SYS:ACCT\BUDGET	MRM	[R W C E M F A]
	Granted to ACCT	[R F]
	ACCT Effective Rights	[R F]
SYS:ACCT\BUDGET\OLD	MRM	[R W C E M F A]
	ACCT Effective Rights	[R F]

This technique affects the ACCT group only. If other groups have rights in these subdirectories, they must be individually restricted.

3.11   NetWare 3.11 maintains an *Inherited Rights Mask (IRM)* for each directory and subdirectory on the server. The IRM is a list of rights that the subdirectory is permitted to inherit from its parent directory. When a directory is created, the IRM is set to allow all rights through, but inherited rights can be reduced or eliminated by restricting rights in the IRM. The IRM does not confer rights; it only controls what rights a directory can inherit.

The IRM intercepts inherited rights both to its own directory and to any subdirectories. Removing a right from the IRM prevents any subdirectories from inheriting that right.

The Inherited Rights Mask is significantly different from the Maximum Rights Mask. The IRM affects subdirectories, and rights can be granted in the directory even though the IRM prevents those rights from being inherited. This example uses the Netware 3.11 Inherited Rights Mask:

SYS:ACCT	IRM	[ ]
	Granted to Group ACCT	[R W C E M F]
	ACCT Effective Rights	[R W C E M F]
SYS:ACCT\BUDGET	IRM	[R F]
	ACCT Effective Rights	[R F]
SYS:ACCT\BUDGET\OLD	IRM	[R W C E M F A]
	ACCT Effective Rights	[R F]

The IRM does not prevent rights from being granted to the ACCT group in SYS:ACCT. The IRM in the BUDGET subdirectory, however, does block the W, C, E, and M rights for both the BUDGET and OLD subdirectories.

The MRM affects rights in its current directory, but does not block the inheritance of rights to subdirectories.

The rights that remain to the user after group, user, and inherited rights are taken into account are the user's *effective rights*.

An example of using the NetWare 3.11 Inherited Rights Mask is incorporated into this directory structure:

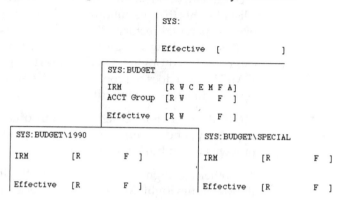

```
                              SYS:

                              Effective   [              ]

               SYS:BUDGET

               IRM          [R W C E M F A]
               ACCT Group   [R W      F  ]

               Effective    [R W      F  ]

SYS:BUDGET\1990                          SYS:BUDGET\SPECIAL

IRM         [R       F  ]                IRM         [R        F  ]

Effective   [R       F  ]                Effective   [R        F  ]
```

The ACCT group has no effective rights at the root level of the SYS: volume, and no rights can be inherited by the subdirectory SYS:BUDGET even though the Inherited Rights Mask does not block any rights.

 Typically, all rights to the volume root directory should be revoked from all users and groups. Rights to subdirectories should be explicitly granted, as required to prevent rights from accidently slipping through from the root directory because they were not masked out.

SYS:BUDGET contains budget files for the current year. Because they are in the process of continuous revision, all members of group ACCT have been given [R W F] rights so that they can read and modify the files. Because no rights were inherited, the effective rights for members of group ACCT are the same as are granted by the group rights.

The files for 1990 are kept available for reporting purposes, but it is important that the files are not modified. The Inherited Rights Mask is used to filter out all rights except R and F. Members of group ACCT do not inherit the W right from the parent directory and are prohibited from modifying files.

IRM blocks all inherited rights in SYS:BUDGET\SPECIAL. To access this subdirectory, you must be granted rights specifically for the subdirectory.

3.11 NetWare 3.11 assigns an Inherited Rights Mask to each file, which controls the rights the file inherits from the directory. Files inherit the effective rights in a directory unless those rights are restricted by the file IRM or by rights that are explicitly assigned to that file.

Determining Effective Rights

To determine a user's effective rights in a directory, you must know the following:

- The user's individual trustee assignments

- The groups to which the user belongs and the trustee assignments for the group

- The Maximum or Inherited Rights Mask at each level of the subdirectory path

Working through all this information can get quite involved, and it has been shown that significant differences exist between the behavior of the Maximum Rights Mask in NetWare 2.2 and the Inherited Rights Mask in NetWare 3.11. The following example illustrates the effective rights for a group and a user at several levels in a directory structure. This example is almost certainly more complex than you are likely to encounter on a real server. DSMITH is a member of the groups ACCT and EVERYONE. At each level, the chart summarizes the effective rights for DSMITH and for group ACCT.

The following example is is based on Netware 3.11.

SYS:	IRM	[	]
	Grant to Group EVERYONE	[	]
	ACCT Effective Rights	[	]
	DSMITH Effective Rights	[	]

SYS:ACCT	IRM	[R	W	C	E	M	F	A]
	Granted to Group ACCT	[R					F	]
	Granted to User DSMITH	[		C				]
	ACCT Effective Rights	[R					F	]
	DSMITH Effective Rights	[R		C			F	]
SYS:ACCT\BUDGET	IRM	[R					F	]
	Granted to Group ACCT	[R	W		E	M	F	]
	ACCT Effective Rights	[R	W		E	M	F	]
	DSMITH Effective Rights	[R	W		E	M	F	]
SYS:ACCT\BUDGET\OLD	IRM	[R					F	]
	Granted to User DSMITH	[R		C			F	]
	ACCT Effective Rights	[R					F	]
	DSMITH Effective Rights	[R		C			F	]
SYS:ACCT\BUDGET\ OLD\REPORTS	IRM	[						]
	Granted to User DSMITH	[R	W	C	E	M	F	A]
	ACCT Effective Rights	[						]
	DSMITH Effective Rights	[R	W	C	E	M	F	A]

At each level, notice that DSMITH's effective rights are the sum of his individual rights and his rights as a member of ACCT.

This scenario works as presented when the NetWare 2.2 Maximum Rights Mask is substituted for the IRM if an MRM is defined at each level, guaranteeing that the desired rights are set at each level.

Read Only vs Read Write Files

Although Read Only and Read Write status are assigned by file attributes, not by trustee assignments, the Ro flag often serves an important security function because it can be used to prevent individual files from being deleted, modified, or renamed.

Some applications insist that program and data files reside in the same directory. To modify data, users must be given Write privileges in the directory. The users also may need Create and Erase privileges because some applications create and delete temporary files during the course of their operation.

To tighten up security, you can flag the program files as Ro, thereby preventing users from accidentally erasing them.

2.2 | Because NetWare version 2.2 cannot assign rights to individual files, using the Ro flag is the only method for restricting modifications to single files. Be sure that users do not have the M right, however, if you want to restrict their ability to reflag the files.

Tasks

Creating Users

Purpose

This task shows you the way in which you can create new users on the network by using the NetWare SYSCON utility. Later tasks describe more detailed features of a NetWare user ID.

Steps

1. Log in as the supervisor.

2. From the command line, enter **SYSCON**.

3. Select **User Information**.

   A list of existing users displays.

4. Press Ins.

   The **User Name** box appears.

5. Enter the new user's login ID.

   To create a user named DSMITH, for example, enter

   DSMITH

   After you press Enter, the box **Path to Create User's Home Directory** displays. The default entry creates all home directories at the root level of SYS:. It is preferable to group these directories under a HOME directory or volume.

6. To place the user's home subdirectories under a \HOME directory, edit the file path to read as follows:

   SYS:HOME\DSMITH

7. After you edit the file path, press Enter to accept the new entry.

   You return to the **User Names** list.

8. Press Enter to select the user ID.

   The **User Information** menu displays. You can enter or modify all user information from this menu. The menu is illustrated in Figure 2.1.

9. Select **Trustee Directory Assignments**. Examine the list of trustee assignments. By now, two entries should exist:

```
SYS:HOME/DSMITH      [RWCEMFA]

SYS:HOME/2200AD      [RWCEMF ]
```

These directories are described in the Notes at the end of this task. You can add additional directory trustee assignments for this user from the **Trustee Directory Assignments** box.

After you complete your examination, press Esc to return to the **User Information** menu.

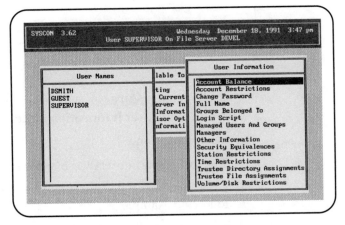

Figure 2.1: The User Information Menu in SYSCON.

10. Select **Account Restrictions**.

    The **Account Restrictions** box is used to enter most of the basic information about a user's account.

11. Enter the desired data in the entry fields. These fields are described in the Notes following this task.

    Figure 2.2 shows an Account Restrictions box that contains suggested entries. See the Notes section for a list of all the fields on this screen.

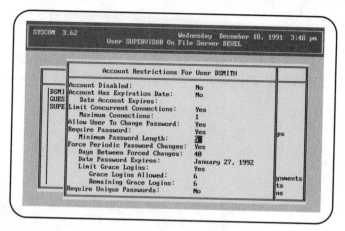

Figure 2.2: Example User Account Restrictions in SYSCON.

12. After you make all desired changes, press Esc to return to the **User Information** menu.

13. Select **Full Name**.

    The **Full Name** entry box is blank for a new user.

14. Enter the user's full name in any format, as in the following example:

    ```
    Smith, David
    ```

    This full name is primarily informational, although it can be displayed at login time with proper commands in the login scripts. It may also be used to index an electronic mail system. For this reason, the sample name is listed last name first. If you use this format, an electronic mail system can index the new user by their last name.

    Press Enter to return to the **User Information** menu.

15. Select **Change Password** to display the **Enter New Password** box. Give the user a generic password that has expired.

    After the user logs in using this password, he or she is asked to change it.

16. Type an initial password in the box, such as **XXXX**, and then press Enter.

17. After the **Retype New Password** box displays, retype the password and press Enter.

You then return to the **User Information** menu.

18. Choose **Account Restrictions**, and examine the **Date Password Expires** entry.

The date shown should indicate that the password has expired. If the password has expired, the new user is forced to change it at the first login attempt.

19. Press Esc. You now can quit SYSCON if desired.

Notes

The **Account Restrictions** box contains the following fields:

- **Account Disabled.** For the account to be functional, this option must be set to **No**. You can disable the account by changing the field to **Yes**, which is useful if an employee has gone on extended leave or if an account is kept available for the occasional use of a contract programmer.

- **Date Account Expires.** You can specify a date after which the account ceases to be available. This field is useful for setting up temporary employees.

- **Limit Concurrent Connections.** This field usually is set to **Yes**, which restricts users to logging in from one workstation at a time. The system supervisor is often the only user without a connection limit.

- **Maximum Connections.** If concurrent connections are limited in the **Limit Concurrent Connections** field, you can set a connection limit of one or more.

- **Allow User to Change Passwords.** If you want passwords to be maintained centrally, change this field to **No**. Users usually are asked to change their own passwords.

- **Require Password.** A password should be required from most users. Occasionally, you may need to set up accounts that do not require passwords. If you do set up an account with no password, make sure that it is restricted by providing it with very limited trustee assignments.

- **Minimum Password Length.** Passwords shorter than five characters are easy to guess. The NetWare SECURITY program, discussed later in this chapter, reports all accounts that have passwords with five or fewer characters. Specify a high minimum password length because longer passwords are more secure.

- **Force Periodic Password Changes.** Passwords become less secure with time and should be changed fairly often.

- **Days Between Force Changes.** The default forty days is a good compromise. Shorten it for better security; lengthen it for greater user convenience.

- **Date Password Expires.** Specify the date the user will next be asked to change his or her password. To expire the password, change the date so that it is prior to today. New users usually are given an expired password that they must change when they first log in.

- **Limit Grace Logins.** Unless this field is set to **Yes**, users can log in indefinitely with expired passwords.

- **Grace Logins Allowed.** This number reflects the number of times a user is allowed to log in with an expired password. This field is available only if **Limit Grace Logins** is set to **Yes**.

- **Remaining Grace Logins.** This number is decreased each time a user logs in with an expired password. When the number reaches zero, the user account is disabled. Supervisors can increase the number to enable locked users to log in and change their passwords.

- **Require Unique Passwords.** Unique passwords are preferable because they cannot be repeated until the password has changed several times. Users often repeat the same password or select from a small number of passwords.

While creating a user, SYSCON creates the user's home directory and gives the user all rights in that directory. SYSCON also creates a mail directory for the user. The number for your new directory differs from the example that was shown earlier because the mail directory numbers are drawn from the user's new ID number, which is created automatically when a new user is created.

Conventions for User Names

If your organization is small, almost any method for assigning user names will function. As more users are created, you should establish some standards for login names.

User names often are used to address electronic mail. They also are used by members of a group that share directories. The most commonly recommended method of defining user names is based on a compromise between using the full user name and the eight-character limit on the login name length.

A good standard for distinguishing among users is to create names based on the user's first initial and six characters of his or her last name. When identical names occur, add a a digit as the eighth character, as in these examples:

Daniel Smith	DSMITH
Laura Sanders	LSANDER1
Larry Sanderson	LSANDER2

Changing Passwords in SYSCON

Purpose

SYSCON enables supervisors and users to change their password.

Steps

1. Start SYSCON.

2. Select **User Information** from the **Available Topics** menu.

3. Select from the user list the user whose password you want to change.

   SYSCON displays the **User Information** menu.

4. Choose **Change Password**.

5. If you are a user, type your old password and press Enter.

6. Enter the new password and press Enter.

7. Reenter the new password for verification and press Enter.

8. Press Esc to return to the **User Information** menu. Exit SYSCON if desired.

Notes

SYSCON manages user-made changes differently from those made by the supervisor:

- Supervisors can change the password for any user. After the change, the password expiration date is set to expire the password.

- Users can change only their own passwords. The password expiration date is set in the future by a number of days assigned in the **Days Between Forced Changes** field in the **User Information** box.

SYSCON does not synchronize passwords if the user attaches to multiple servers. On multiserver networks, use the SETPASS command line utility.

Changing Your Password with SETPASS

Purpose

Use the SETPASS command line utility to change your password. If you have accounts on several servers, the SETPASS command is the best way to change your password because it can synchronize your password on all attached servers.

If a menu is used to support access to LAN applications, users will find it helpful if a **Change Password** menu option accesses SETPASS.

Steps

The following steps assume that user DSMITH has logged in to server FS1 and must attach to server FS2.

1. Log in.

   If the login procedure does not attach you automatically to all required servers, you must attach manually to each server. The following sample lines illustrate this procedure:

   ```
   F:\>ATTACH FS2
   Username: DSMITH
   Password: user enters password for FS2
   ```

2. From the DOS prompt, enter

   SETPASS

3. Enter your old password at the prompt.

4. Enter your new password twice for verification.

5. Respond **Yes** when asked if passwords should be synchronized on all attached servers.

6. Log in to test the new ID.

Notes

The following sample lines illustrate the SETPASS procedure:

```
F:\LOGIN>WHOAMI
You are user DSMITH attached to server FS1, connection 1.
Server FS1 is running Dedicated NetWare V2.2(50) Rev. A.
Login time: Tuesday December 10, 1991 1:54 pm
F:\LOGIN>ATTACH FS2/DSMITH
Password:user enters password for FS2
You are attached to server FS2.
F:\LOGIN>SETPASS
Enter old password for FS1/DSMITH:
Enter new password for FS1/DSMITH:
Retype new password for FS1/DSMITH:
The password for FS1/DSMITH has been changed.
Synchronize passwords on these file servers with FS1/DSMITH? (Y/N) Y
The password for FS2/DSMITH has been changed.
F:\LOGIN>
```

 Do not forget your supervisor password. If you forget or lose your password, you must get professional technical assistance to get back into the system.

Selecting Passwords

People often choose a password that others can guess. Passwords based on the names of relatives, loved ones, hobbies, phone numbers, Social Security numbers, or birth dates are easy to guess if someone tries to get into your account.

Follow these suggestions when you create passwords:

- Use long passwords rather than short passwords. Others can learn your password by watching you type your password at your workstation. A long password is less detectable.

- Use a combination of numbers and letters when you create a password.

- Use nonsense passwords, such as X275HYN, because they are hard to guess. These passwords also are hard to remember, but you can create a nonsense sentence such as "Cross out two from seven, then five have you now" to help you remember each character.

- Another way to create safe passwords is to combine two words that are separated by a punctuation mark. A few examples are MY_KEY, PAPER.SNOW, and BELL&CANDLE.

- Never write down your password because it will no longer be safe. Remember that if you forget your password, your supervisor can reassign a new password that you can change. The supervisor password, however, should be known by at least two people in the company to ensure that network data is still accessible.

- Change your password every 60 days.

The supervisor can require a minimum password length and can set an automatic expiration date for passwords. These features should be considered basic security, and should be implemented on a server to protect valuable company information.

NetWare cannot determine whether users are using secure passwords. For this reason, system administrators who must ensure extremely high levels of security may choose to assign all passwords centrally. User accounts can be set to require passwords that the user cannot change. With this system, the administrator assigns passwords that meet specific security guidelines. In extreme situations, passwords might be randomly generated by a computer program. The password X93S2Z, for example, is difficult to remember, but it is also difficult to guess.

Controlling the User's Maximum Connections

Purpose

This task shows you the way in which you can limit the number of simultaneous times a user can be logged on to his or her account.

Limiting simultaneous network connections avoids application conflicts. NetWare-compatible applications often use the same subdirectories for work files and do not work correctly if they are run more than once at the same time by the same user name.

Steps

1. Log in as a supervisor.

2. Start SYSCON.

3. From the **Available Topics** menu, select **User Information**.

   The system responds with the **User Names** list.

4. Select the name of the user that you want to restrict, and then press Enter.

   SYSCON responds with the **User Information** menu.

5. From the **User Information** menu, select **Account Restrictions**.

6. On the **Account Restrictions** box, select the **Limit Concurrent Connections** field, then enter **Y**.

7. In the **Maximum Connections** field, enter the maximum number of connections that you want for this user.

8. Press **Esc** to save the changes.

9. Exit SYSCON if desired.

Note

Some programs create temporary work files, temporary work directories, or both, in the current directory. These programs do not run properly if run by the same user at more than one workstation at a time. Limiting users to a single login per ID usually avoids such software problems. If users must be able to access such applications simultaneously from several workstations, you need to develop procedures to circumvent these problems. Often it is easier to give the user a second login ID.

Limiting a User to Specific Workstations

Purpose

Use the workstation network address to limit users to specific workstations. Suppose that you set up a user named BACKUP who is responsible for performing all tape backup operations. This user must have supervisor privileges to access NetWare security information, and anyone learning the password for this user would have supervisor access to the server. You can restrict the BACKUP user to the workstation that is equipped with the tape drive, which should be located in a secure area. Even though a user may discover the password for BACKUP, access is restricted unless the user has physical access to the backup PC.

Steps

1. Create the user to be restricted.

2. Log in to the workstation to which this user will be restricted.

3. To find the network and node address for this station, type **USERLIST/A**.

   Examine the workstation list for the line that is flagged with an asterisk.

   Make a note of the Network and the Node Address for the starred workstation. These unique addresses identify the workstation from which you logged in.

4. From the DOS prompt, enter **SYSCON.**

5. From the **Available Topics** menu, select **User Information**.

6. From the **User Names** menu, select the name of the user that you want to restrict.

7. From the **User Information** menu, select **Station Restrictions**.

8. In the **Allowed Login Address** panel, press Ins to display the **Network Address** field.

9. Enter the network address for the selected workstation, as recorded in Step 2.

10. At the `Allow Login From All Nodes` prompt, type **N** to select **No**.

11. Enter the node address for the selected workstation, as recorded in Step 2.

12. Press Esc and quit SYSCON if desired.

Limiting User Disk Space with SYSCON

Purpose

Use the SYSCON utility to set storage limits. The DSPACE utility provides another way to limit a user's storage on particular volumes. See the next task for information about DSPACE.

2.2	NetWare 2.2 limits user storage for the entire server, regardless of the number or configuration of volumes.

3.11	Netware 3.11 establishes storage limits individually for each volume.

Steps

1. From the DOS prompt, enter **SYSCON.**

2. From the **Available Topics** menu, select **User Information**.

3. From the **User Names** menu, select the name of the user that you want to restrict.

4. From the **User Information** menu, select **Volume / Disk Restrictions**.

5. If the server version is 3.11, select a volume from the list that is presented.

6. The **User Volume/Disk Restrictions** box is displayed.

7. Change the **Limit Volume/Server Space** to Yes.

8. Change the **Volume Space Limit/Maximum Server Disk Space** to the limit you select in kilobytes.

9. Press Esc and quit SYSCON if desired.

Notes

2.2   Before you can set storage limits in NetWare 2.2, you must use the INSTALL utility to set the **Limit disk space** option. See the Appendix for this procedure.

In step 5 of the Appendix, edit the following configuration items as shown:

```
Limit disk space:          Yes
Maximum bindery objects:   1500
```

The number of bindery objects limits the number of users and groups that can be defined on the file server. Your configuration may require more or less bindery objects than shown. This value has a range of 500 through 5000. 1500 is the default value.

Limiting Storage Allocations with DSPACE

Purpose

Use the DSPACE utility as an alternative utility for limiting the space available to a user on each volume.

| 2.2 | NetWare 2.2 limits user storage for the entire server, regardless of the number or configuration of volumes. |

| 3.11 | Netware 3.11 establishes storage limits individually for each volume. |

Steps

1. Run DSPACE.

2. Select **User Restrictions**.

3. Select the ID of the user that you want to limit from the list.

4. If using NetWare 3.11, select the volume that you want to limit.

5. Highlight the **Limit Space** field and type Y.

6. Highlight the **Available** field and enter **2048**.

   Adjust this number to establish the desired limitations.

7. Press Esc.

   You have limited the storage allocation for DSMITH on volume SYS: to 2 megabytes.

Note

You must configure NetWare 2.2 by using INSTALL before you can enter disk space limitations. See "Limiting User Disk Space with SYSCON" for instructions.

Limiting User Login Times

Purpose

This task enables you to set time restrictions for user logins.

Limiting access times to the server ensures that unauthorized personnel with a user password cannot access a user's account after the user's designated login hours. Limiting user login times also is useful if you perform unattended tape backups and you want to ensure that users are logged out of the network during backups.

Steps

1. Log in as the supervisor.

2. From the DOS prompt, enter **SYSCON**.

   The system displays the **Available Topics** menu.

3. From the **Available Topics** menu, select **User Information**.

4. From the **User Names** list, use the cursor keys to select the name of the user for whom you want to assign access times, then press Enter.

5. From the **User Information** menu, select **Time Restrictions**.

   The **Allowed Login Times For User** panel is displayed. An example is shown in Figure 2.3.

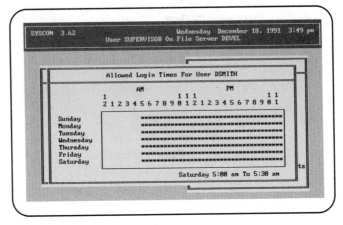

Figure 2.3: Example Login Time Restrictions.

6. Enter asterisks in the time slots that match the times for user access. Press the spacebar to remove asterisks from time slots for which you want to restrict user access.

Figure 2.3 shows that access is denied between 12:00 midnight and 5:00 a.m., the period when tape backups are performed.

7. Press Esc to save the values.

8. Exit SYSCON if desired.

Notes

A message displays if an attempt is made to log in during hours that are not included in the allotted time slots, as in the following example:

```
F:\LOGIN>LOGIN DSMITH
FS1/DSMITH:Attempting to login during an unauthorized time period.
The supervisor has limited the times that you can login to this
server.
```

If a user remains logged in past an allotted time slot, NetWare issues the following warning:

```
>>FS1 CONNECTION TIME EXPIRED. PLEASE LOG OUT. (CTRL-ENTER To Clear)
```

If the warning appears, the user must press Ctrl-Enter, quickly save any work, and then log out. If this procedure is not followed, the system attempts to "correct" the situation by clearing the station, which may close incomplete data files.

Setting time restrictions for users is slow because of the number of required keystrokes. If you change the time restrictions, you must change time restrictions for each user on the network. To avoid this irritation, plan carefully your needs for time restrictions. Follow the steps in the task "Setting Default User Parameters" to set up default time restrictions.

Setting Default User Parameters

Purpose

Use the SYSCON utility to create a default set of parameters for new users that are added to the network.

System administrators frequently add new users to a network. Most new users share common characteristics, that can be included in a default set of user parameters using the SYSCON utility.

Steps

1. Log in as the supervisor.

2. From the command line, run SYSCON.

3. Select **Supervisor Options**.

4. Select **Default Account Balance/Restrictions**.

5. Enter the desired default values and press Esc.

6. Select **Default Time Restrictions**.

7. Enter asterisks in the time slots that match the times for user access. Press the spacebar to remove asterisks from time slots for which you want to restrict user access, and then press Esc.

8. Press Esc to accept the times displayed. Quit SYSCON if desired.

Using SYSCON To Maintain User Trustee Rights

Purpose

Supervisors and users having Access Control rights can use the SYSCON menu utility to change NetWare trustee rights for users.

Steps

1. Log in as the supervisor.

2. From the DOS prompt, enter **SYSCON**.

3. From the **Available Topics** menu, select **User Information**.

4. From the **User Names** menu, select an existing user.

5. From the **User Information** menu, use the cursor keys to select **Trustee Directory Assignments**, then press Enter.

    After you press Enter, the current trustee directory assignments are displayed.

6. Press Ins to add a new directory.

7. At the prompt for `Directory In Which Trustee Should Be Added`, type the volume name, a colon, and the subdirectory path.

    You also can use menus to select the directory that is to be modified. Press Ins to bring up the first menu. Press Enter to select items from menus. Press Esc after the path is complete.

    Press Enter to accept the directory path.

8. Select the desired directory and press Enter.

    Current trustee rights for the directory are displayed. If this is a new trustee assignment, the default rights of [R F] are listed.

9. Highlight rights and press Del to remove rights.

10. Press Ins to add attributes. Select an attribute from the displayed list and press Enter. Or select several attributes by highlighting them with F5; then press Enter to select the highlighted attributes.

11. Press Esc to accept the assignment.

12. Exit SYSCON if desired.

Notes

> **3.11** In NetWare 3.11, you can use a procedure that is similar to the steps in this task to assign rights to files. Use the **Trustee File Assignments** option from the **User Information** menu. You will be asked to select a directory path followed by a file within the directory.
>
> SYSCON and FILER support the assignment of trustee rights, but they force you to assign rights one file at a time, which is often a slow process. A faster method is to use the GRANT command. See the task "Managing File and Directory Rights with GRANT" for more information on GRANT.

Using SYSCON To Create and Maintain Group Rights

Purpose

Supervisors and users having Access Control rights can use the SYSCON menu utility to list and change group NetWare trustee rights.

Steps

1. Log in as the supervisor.

2. From the DOS prompt, enter **SYSCON**.

3. From the **Available Topics** menu, select **Group Information**.

To create a new group, proceed with steps 4 and 5. To modify an existing group, skip to step 6.

4. To create a new group, press Ins in the **Group Names** menu. Then type the new group's name and press Enter. You will be returned to the **Group Names** menu.

5. Select a group from the list.

6. From the **Group Information** menu, use the cursor keys to select **Trustee Directory Assignments**, then press Enter.

   After you press Enter, the current trustee directory assignments display.

7. Press Ins if you want to create a new directory.

8. At the prompt for **Directory In Which Trustee Should Be Added**, edit the directory path as required.

   You also can use menus to select the directory that is to be modified. Press Ins to bring up the first menu. Press Enter to select items from menus. Press Esc when the path is complete.

   Press Enter to accept the directory path.

9. Select the desired directory and press Enter.

   Current trustee rights display. If this is a new trustee assignment, the default rights of [R F] are listed.

10. Highlight rights and press Del to remove rights.

11. Press Ins to add attributes. Select an attribute from the displayed list and press Enter. Or select several attributes by highlighting them with F5; then press Enter to select the highlighted attributes.

12. Press Esc to return to the **Group Information** box.

13. If you want to modify the list of users who are members of the group, select the **Member List**.

    The group user list displays.

14. To delete a user, highlight the login name and press Del.

15. To delete several users, highlight each user then press the F5 key. Afterward, press Del when all users are marked.

16. To add users, press Ins to display a list of users not already in the group.

17. To add a user to the group, highlight the name and press Enter.

18. To add several users, highlight each name then press the F5 key. Afterward, press Enter when all users are marked.

19. Press Esc when all user changes have been made. You will return to the **Group Information** menu.

20. Exit SYSCON if desired.

Notes

3.11 In NetWare 3.11, assigning rights to files is similar to assigning rights to directories. Use the **Trustee File Assignments** from the **Group Information** menu. You are asked to select a directory path followed by a file within the directory. Assigning rights to files may be faster when you use the GRANT command because the SYSCON forces you to assign rights one file at a time. See the task "Managing Rights with GRANT" for more information on the GRANT command.

 You can also grant group membership when defining users in SYSCON. Use the **Groups Belonged To** option in the **User Information** menu to add single users. If you want to change memberships of several users in a group, it usually is faster to use the **Member List** option in the **Group Information** menu of SYSCON as described in this task.

Managing Rights Using GRANT

Purpose

Supervisors and users having Access Control rights can use the GRANT command line utility to manage trustee assignments. In some situations, using GRANT is more convenient than using FILER because GRANT accepts wild cards in path arguments.

Steps

To assign multiple rights to the group ACCT in the current directory, separate each right with a space, as in the command:

```
GRANT R W C E F TO ACCT
```

The GRANT command requires at least the following information:

- The rights to be granted. Use the letters that represent the rights, separated by spaces. See Tables 2.1 and 2.2 for descriptions of the various trustee rights and their letter abbreviations.

- The group or user to receive the trustee assignment.

    It can be considerably quicker to make trustee assignments with GRANT than to step through the various menu levels in SYSCON.

Notes

The rights given by GRANT usually are in addition to any already held by the user. The first statement below gives DSMITH R and F rights. The second statement adds the W right. After these statements, DSMITH has R, W, and F rights.

```
GRANT R F TO DSMITH
GRANT W TO DSMITH
```

If you are granting every right to a group, specify ALL in the rights list instead of typing every right:

```
GRANT ALL TO ACCT
```

ACCT now has rights R, W, C, E, F, M, and A in the current directory.

To remove rights, use N (for "None") in the rights list. To revoke all rights in the current directory from group ACCT, enter:

```
GRANT N TO ACCT
```

The rights list can contain ALL, N, or any combination of rights key letters.

The recipient of a rights assignment can be either a user or a group. The previous examples that granted rights to groups such as ACCT can be substituted with such users as DSMITH.

You can use the ALL, BUT, and ONLY options with the rights list. The ONLY option grants rights specified in the command and revokes any existing rights of the user or group. If the ONLY option is not used in the command, the specified rights are added to any existing rights.

```
GRANT ALL BUT A TO DSMITH
GRANT ONLY R F to ACCT
```

If a group and a user share a name, you must indicate which entity you want to modify by adding a GROUP or a USER keyword:

```
GRANT R W C F TO USER AUDIT
GRANT R W TO GROUP AUDIT
```

To assign rights in a different directory, specify a path:

```
GRANT R F FOR F:\APPS\EDIT TO GROUP EVERYONE
```

Checking Trustee Assignments with TLIST

Purpose

TLIST can be used to check the trustee assignments in a directory.

Steps

Type TLIST to display the trustee assignments in the current directory.

A list of the directory's trustee assignments displays.

Type TLIST SYS:\PUBLIC to display the trustee assignments in SYS:PUBLIC. You can substitute the path for any network directory in this command.

Notes

A TLIST report looks like this:

```
FS1\SYS:SUB1
User trustees:
                        DSMITH   [RWC  F ]
                        — —
Group trustees:
EVERYONE                [RWCEMFA]
```

The TLIST command does not report effective rights. It does not take into account inherited rights or rights masks.

Revoking User and Group Trustee Assignments

Purpose

Supervisors and users who have Access Control rights can use the REMOVE and REVOKE commands for rights maintenance. Use REMOVE to remove completely users or groups from a directory's trustee list.

Use REVOKE to revoke specific rights. This command is the opposite of GRANT.

Steps

The following examples illustrate the use of the REMOVE and REVOKE commands.

To remove group ACCT from the SYS:BUDGET directory, enter:

REMOVE ACCT FROM SYS:BUDGET

Users are removed similarly, as in the command:

REMOVE DSMITH FROM F:UTILITY

If a user and group share the same name, GROUP or USER must be specified. For example:

REMOVE USER AUDIT FROM \AUDIT\1990
REMOVE GROUP AUDIT FROM \AUDIT\1990

Add the /SUB option to remove the group ACCT from subdirectories:

REMOVE ACCT FROM SYS:BUDGET /SUB

REVOKE commands are structured similarly to GRANT commands, as in the following examples:

REVOKE W E F:\ACCT FROM DSMITH
REVOKE ALL SYS:BUDGET FROM GROUP ACCT
REVOKE W C M A \SPRDSHT FROM USER ACCT /SUB

Setting the Directory Inherited/Maximum Rights Mask

Purpose

Users who have Access Control rights for a directory or a file can modify the corresponding Inherited or Maximum Rights Masks. Follow the steps in this task to modify the Inherited and Maximum Rights Masks.

The Maximum Rights Mask is used on NetWare 2.2 servers, while NetWare 3.11 servers use the Inherited Rights Mask. Consult the concepts discussion in this chapter for the distinction between the Maximum and Inherited Rights Masks.

Steps

1. Run **FILER** from the command line.

2. In the **Available Topics** menu, choose **Select Current Directory**.

3. Edit the current directory path or press Ins to use the path insertion technique. Press Enter to accept the directory path and return to the **Available Topics** menu.

4. Select the **Current Directory Information** option.

5. Highlight the **Inherited/Maximum Effective Rights** field and press Enter.

    The current rights will be displayed.

6. To delete rights, highlight the rights and press Del.

7. To add rights, press Ins, highlight the right you want to add, then press Enter.

8. To add more than one right, highlight each right, then press the F5 key. Afterward, press Enter.

9. Press Esc. Quit **FILER** if desired.

Setting the File Inherited Rights Mask in Netware 3.11

Purpose

Follow the steps in this task to modify the Inherited Rights Masks of a file. You must have Access Control rights for a file to modify its Inherited Rights.

Inherited Rights Masks for files are supported by NetWare 3.x only.

Steps

1. Run FILER from the command line.

2. In the **Available Topics** menu, choose **Select Current Directory**.

3. Edit the current directory path.

   You also can use menus to select the directory that is to be modified. Press Ins to bring up the first menu. Press Enter to select items from menus. Press Esc when the path is complete.

   Press Enter to accept the directory path.

   After you press Enter, you return to the **Available Topics** menu.

4. Select the **Directory Contents** option in the **Available Topics** menu.

5. Highlight the file you want to modify, then press Enter.

6. Select **View/Set File Information**.

   The file information screen displays.

7. Highlight the **Inherited Rights Mask** field, then press Enter to display the current list of rights.

8. To delete rights, highlight the rights and press Del.

9. To add rights, press Ins, highlight a desired right, then press Enter.

   To select several rights, highlight each right that you want to add and press the F5 key. Afterward, press Enter.

10. Press Esc. Quit FILER if desired.

Determining Effective Rights

Purpose

The RIGHTS command displays a user's effective rights for any directory.

When you need to determine a user's effective rights, the RIGHTS command is easier to use than the process of examining trustee rights and directory masks.

Steps

1. Log in as the user to be checked.

2. Change to the directory for which you want to view the user's effective rights and enter the command:

   RIGHTS

Notes

After you enter the RIGHTS command, a report similar to the following displays:

```
FS1\SYS:HOME/DSMITH
Your Effective Rights for this directory are [RWCEMFA]
     May Read from File.                         (R)
     May Write to File.                          (W)
     May Create Subdirectories and Files.
     May Erase Subdirectories and Files.
     May Modify File Status Flags.               (M)
     May Scan for Files.                         (F)
     May Change Access Control.                  (A)
     You have ALL RIGHTS to this directory area.
```

Using Security Equivalence

Purpose

This task shows you how to define one user's security privileges in terms of another user.

Steps

1. Log in as the supervisor.

2. From the DOS prompt, enter **SYSCON**.

3. From the **Available Topics** menu, select **User Information**.

4. From the **User Names** menu, select a user.

5. From the **User Information** menu, select **Security Equivalences**.

   The **Security Equivalences** panel is displayed.

6. Press Ins.

7. From the **Other Users & Groups** list, select a user or group to whom the current user is to be made equivalent, then press Enter.

8. To make a user a system supervisor, select SUPERVISOR (USER) from the **Other Users & Groups** list.

9. Press Esc. Quit SYSCON if desired.

Notes

Setting the security level of one user to that of another user is helpful in the following situations:

- If a guest user will be active only a short time. Security equivalence may be a good way to define rights for the guest's account.

- If a user's trustee rights are not functioning as required, the supervisor can create a temporary user and assign the temporary user the same security as the problem user. The supervisor can then examine the user's directories using the same rights and the RIGHTS command to see if trustee assignments are as expected. Without using this technique, the Supervisor must log in as the problem user and must know that user's password.

- If additional system administrators are to function as supervisors, they must given security equivalence to the SUPERVISOR user ID. If several users are to administer the system, each user should have a personal ID. This ID will be used as an owner stamp on files, which simplifies the process of tracing system changes to the administrator who made them.

A disadvantage of security equivalence is that the rights definitions disappear when the pattern user is deleted. Group and individual assignments are more reliable ways to assign rights to long-term user accounts.

 For a user to have full supervisory privileges, he or she also must be made a Console Operator. In SYSCON, access **Supervisor Options/File Server Console Operators**. Press Ins to select a new console operator from the user list.

Using Encrypted Passwords

Purpose

Encrypt user passwords to ensure that they remain secure.

If all your servers are running Netware 2.12 or above, follow the steps in this task to configure your network for encrypted passwords.

Steps

If any of your servers are running Netware 3.x, follow these steps:

1. On the server console command screen, type

   `SET ALLOW UNENCRYPTED PASSWORDS`

   The console displays the current value of this parameter. To support encrypted passwords, the value must be OFF.

2. If **Allow Unencrypted Passwords** is ON, type the command:

   `SET ALLOW UNENCRYPTED PASSWORDS=OFF`

3. If **Allow Unencrypted Passwords** was set to ON, it may be due to a line in the AUTOEXEC.NCF file. Use the INSTALL utility to check the AUTOEXEC.NCF file for this SET statement, and remove it if it exists.

Netware 2.2 always works with encrypted passwords. If any of your servers are running Netware 2.1x, however, the Netware 3.x utilities must be copied to those servers. Assume in the following steps that a Netware 3.x server named FS1 is available:

1. Log in to the 2.1x server.

2. Flag files in the PUBLIC and LOGIN directories as Shareable Read Write by typing

   FLAG SYS:PUBLIC SRW
   FLAG SYS:LOGIN SRW

3. Attach to the 3.*x* server by typing

   ATTACH PS1/SUPERVISOR

4. Enter the supervisor password when prompted.

5. To copy the utilities from a 3.*x* server named PS1, type the following commands:

   NCOPY FS1/SYS:PUBLIC SYS:PUBLIC
   NCOPY FS1/SYS:LOGIN SYS:LOGIN

6. Flag the copied files as shareable read-only by typing

   FLAG SYS:PUBLIC SRO
   FLAG SYS:LOGIN SRO

7. Repeat this procedure for each 2.1x server.

Notes

Information travels over the network in IPX/SPX packages, otherwise known as *data packets*. An increasing number of applications are capable of capturing raw NetWare data packets as they travel over network cabling. These applications enable users to view data as it moves over the network cables, bypassing any security. With the right software and hardware, users can capture and decode packets containing user passwords.

By encrypting passwords, you prevent intruders from scanning user passwords, which are the foundations of a secure network. Encrypted passwords also prevent applications from "sniffing" or determining passwords over a network.

 Note that all NetWare servers on a particular LAN must have the same configuration for password encryption. Netware 2.1*x*, 2.2, and 3.*x* can coexist if encryption is enabled. Do not use encrypted passwords on networks that include NetWare versions earlier than 2.12 because these versions cannot support password encryption.

Checking System Security

Purpose

Use the NetWare SECURITY program to identify security errors that may be overlooked when you set up a network. The NetWare security program checks every user account for configuration errors that may lead to security breaches.

Steps

1. Log in as the system supervisor.

2. At the DOS prompt, change to the SYSTEM directory by entering:

   CD \SYSTEM

3. At the DOS prompt, enter

   SECURITY

   After you press Enter, the system responds by checking the following network areas: bindery user objects, supervisor managers, managed users and groups, mail directories, and standard directories (SYSTEM, PUBLIC, LOGIN, and MAIL).

The SECURITY utility checks every area of a network for excessive rights and other mistakes. *Excessive rights* include any extra unsecure rights given to named objects.

The SECURITY program report can identify the following conditions in a user account:

- No password assigned
- An unsecure password
- No password required
- Passwords that are too short (fewer than five letters)
- Passwords with an expiration interval greater than 60 days
- Periodic password changes are not required
- Unique passwords are not required
- Security equivalent to the SUPERVISOR
- No log-in script
- No mail directory
- Account has been disabled
- Account has not been used for more than three weeks
- No full name specified
- No holes in security detected

Many basic security holes are easily overlooked when you set up a NetWare LAN or perform maintenance on existing user accounts. Common security mistakes include forgetting to assign a password or assigning a password with too few letters. Short passwords are easier to guess using password-deciphering programs.

Securing the Network Using Intruder Detection

Purpose

This task enables you to protect your network from unwanted intruders. Intruder detection locks an account when a specified number of unsuccessful login attempts have been made.

Steps

1. Log in as the system supervisor.

2. From the DOS prompt, enter **SYSCON**.

   The system displays the SYSCON **Available Options** menu.

3. From the **Available Options** menu, use the cursor keys to select **Supervisor Options** and then press Enter.

4. From the **Supervisor Options** menu, use the cursor keys to select **Intruder Detection/Lockout**.

5. On the **Intruder Detection/Lockout** screen panel, press **Y** to turn on the **Detect Intruders** option.

   The system responds by displaying the default intruder detection settings, which permit seven incorrect log-in attempts within a 30-minute period. You can change the default values to any combination.

6. Enter the number of incorrect log-in attempts permitted before a user's account is locked out. You can specify any number greater than zero.

7. After you press Enter, you are prompted to enter the **Bad Login Count Retention Time**. The system remembers incorrect log-in attempts for the amount of time you specify in days, hours, and minutes. For this task, enter **0** for Days, **0** for Hours, and **30** for Minutes.

The default permits seven incorrect login attempts within a 30-minute period. You can change the default values to any combination.

8. At the **Lock Account After Detection** prompt, enter **Y** to enable locking of the user account after an intruder is detected.

9. Next, you are prompted to enter the **Length of Account Lockout**. Enter the number of days, hours, and minutes the account will remain locked out. For this task, enter **0** for Days, **0** for Hours, and **15** for Minutes.

    Any failed login attempt over the threshold count locks the user's account for 15 minutes, even if the correct password is eventually supplied.

10. Press Esc to accept the new entries. Quit SYSCON if desired.

Notes

Experienced users can write programs that run through thousands (or even tens of thousands) of passwords per hour. If such programs are left running over a weekend, they may guess your password. Intruder detection slows this trial-and-error process considerably.

After an account is locked out, the user cannot log in until the set time period has expired or a user with supervisor rights re-enables the account.

Repairing the NetWare Bindery

Purpose

This task shows you how to use the BINDFIX utility to maintain and repair the NetWare bindery.

Steps

1. Log in as a supervisor.

2. Ask all users to log out of the server.

   Users are unable to log in while BINDFIX executes.

3. Switch to the SYS:SYSTEM directory.

4. Enter the command

   BINDFIX

5. Respond to the BINDFIX prompts.

6. Review the rebuilt bindery to ensure that it is correct.

7. If the rebuilt bindery is damaged, NetWare makes a copy of the old bindery that you can restore by entering the command

   BINDREST

8. If you are satisfied that the rebuilt bindery is correct, you can delete the old versions of the bindery file by typing

   DEL F:\SYSTEM*.OLD

Notes

The *bindery* consists of three files that NetWare uses to store information about users, groups, file servers, print servers, and other named entities. The following files, which are stored in the SYS:SYSTEM directory, contain bindery data:

- **NET$OBJ.SYS**. Stores information about objects. Objects consist of named entities.

- **NET$PROP.SYS**. Stores the characteristics or properties of the various objects.

- **NET$VAL.SYS**. Stores property data.

Information in these files is updated by such NetWare utilities as SYSCON and FILER. Occasionally, the bindery becomes corrupted. Your bindery files may be corrupted if you experience any of the following problems:

- Passwords cannot be changed.

- Users cannot be deleted.

- Rights cannot be deleted or modified.

- Error messages mention the bindery.

Follow the steps in this task to access and repair the bindery files.

Protecting the Network from Viruses

A computer virus is a serious threat to local area networks, especially to networks that consist of many users, many disk drives, and few rules. By following a few basic guidelines, you can detect viruses and protect your system from attack. Use the following guidelines to keep your network safe:

- Make tape backups often. Periodically make a backup and keep it for six months to a year. Some viruses take months to announce their presence.

- Keep your workstation in a low-risk group by limiting outside software sources. One precaution is to limit the number of users who can carry information from the network to a home computer.

- Only install new software contained in shrink-wrapped packages.

- Test any new software before installation and test all hard-disk volumes of a file server with a commercial virus-checking package. These programs find most current viruses and are updated regularly. If these applications are used properly, they can eradicate viruses before they cause any problems. If you own a virus-scanning package, keep it current by obtaining updates from the vendor.

- Avoid running applications if you are logged in as SUPERVISOR or as a user who has the security privileges of a supervisor. Infected software run at the supervisor level is much more capable of spreading computer viruses because the supervisor has rights across the file server.

- Consider the use of diskless workstations to prohibit users from copying information from work to home, and vice versa.

- Do not disregard shareware applications because you think they may be unsafe; simply check the program with a virus test. If you are concerned about shareware applications, ask the application's publisher for a new copy. Run the program in quarantine on a stand-alone PC to see if any time-bombs are present.

- Unless you download software, do not worry about communicating with such information sources as BBS systems, Compuserve, or Prodigy. Data files are rarely the cause of virus infection. Although a piece of software may be "infected," the act of downloading or copying it to your disk does not cause infection; the program must be run to infect your system. For this reason, check downloaded programs for viruses before you execute them.

3

WORKSTATIONS

Proper configuration of the workstation is essential for providing the user with a reliable network working environment. Unless you are fortunate enough to work in an office that has only one brand and configuration of personal computer, coping with individual workstation differences is a fact of life. This chapter equips you with some of the tools you need to configure workstations that work effectively with a Novell network. It examines software issues that arise out of the configuration of DOS and NetWare files on the workstations.

Topics considered in this chapter include:

- Configuring DOS on the workstation to work with a LAN

- Configuring and installing the NetWare IPX.COM file

- Selecting from the various NETx shell file options and configuring the workstation for each shell file type

- Troubleshooting network connections

Key Concepts

The overwhelming number of workstations on NetWare networks run some version of MS-DOS or PC DOS. PC DOS is IBM's brand of DOS. Although some differences between MS-DOS and PC DOS exist, they are essentially identical for the purposes of this book. All versions of MS-DOS use configuration files to initialize the user's working environment. These configuration files also have effects on networking. MS-DOS Version 5.0 is used as the reference for this book.

NetWare adds several of its own files to the workstation. These files contain programs that allow the workstation to communicate through the network to network resources.

In all, five files must be considered. Also to be considered is a feature of DOS called the environment.

The DOS Environment

DOS maintains a part of its memory known as its environment. Within the environment, DOS stores information that is required by DOS services and by application programs. Information in the environment also can be accessed by NetWare.

One item in the environment is PATH. The path is the list of directories in which DOS searches for commands that cannot be found in the current directory. Another item is COMSPEC, which tells DOS which command file to use to interpret the commands that the user types. Other items can be placed in the environment by users or by programs.

The environment initially can hold 160 to 256 bytes of data depending on the DOS version, but the environment size can be increased by a SHELL command in the CONFIG.SYS file.

CONFIG.SYS

One of the first things DOS does when it boots on a workstation is to look for a file named CONFIG.SYS. This file can contain several commands that determine the way in which DOS configures itself for the workstation. CONFIG.SYS is always installed in the root directory of the workstation boot drive.

The following lines typically are found in a CONFIG.SYS file:

```
FILES=20

BUFFERS=20
```

When these commands are encountered during the workstation boot process, DOS configures itself as follows:

- DOS can open as many as 20 workstation files simultaneously (the default is 8). A variety of applications require more than 8 files to execute properly.

- DOS maintains 20 512-byte disk buffers in its system memory (RAM). When DOS reads or writes data to a disk file, the data also is written in the disk buffers. If an attempt is made to read data from disk, DOS first checks to see whether the data is already present in a buffer. Disk buffers speed the retrieval of frequently read data because it is faster to retrieve data from system memory than from disk. Within limits, increasing disk buffers improves PC hard disk performance.

 Increasing DOS buffers does not affect network performance because NetWare diverts all network file services around DOS to the fileserver. If local disk performance is not critical, you can increase memory available to DOS by setting BUFFERS= to a low value, or even using BUFFERS=1 in CONFIG.SYS.

Other DOS commands of interest that are found in CONFIG.SYS files include the following:

DEVICE=   Loads device drivers. Device drivers are frequently used to install memory managers. Common examples include HIMEM.SYS and SMARTDRV.SYS, which are shipped with MS-DOS 5.0.

LASTDRIVE=   Informs DOS how many disk drives are present. DOS usually assumes that five disk drives are present, which are named A: through E:.

SHELL=   Changes features of the user command environment.

The implications of each of these commands for NetWare is examined later in this chapter.

AUTOEXEC.BAT

The last thing DOS does when it boots is to look for a file named AUTOEXEC.BAT in the root directory of the boot drive. Any DOS commands found in this file are executed. An AUTOEXEC.BAT file suitable for a network workstation is presented later in this chapter.

IPX.COM

The IPX.COM NetWare file provides the communication link between the workstation's software and the NetWare server. IPX.COM performs these functions:

- It communicates between the workstation software and the network interface card. The NetWare WSGEN utility is used to customize IPX.COM for each brand and model of network card.

- It communicates between the workstation network card and the NetWare server. IPX.COM supports the *communications protocols* named IPX (Internetwork Packet Exchange) and SPX (Sequenced Package Exchange). A communication protocol is a set of rules for sending data over a network. These rules make sure that data arrives at the intended destinations.

NETx.COM

NETx.COM actually represents a group of programs. One of these programs is selected for use on the workstation to provide the NetWare *shell*, which is so called because it forms a shell around DOS and NetWare and is the first software to receive user and program requests for DOS and NetWare services.

The NetWare shell examines all command requests that take place in the workstation to determine whether they call for local or network resources. Local requests, such as a request for a directory on C:, are sent to DOS. Server requests are sent to the server via the server communication link that is provided by IPX.COM.

A version of NETx.COM exists for each revision level of DOS. The x in NETx is replaced with a number between 2 and 5, depending on the DOS version that runs on the workstation. A workstation running MS-DOS Version 5.0, for example, uses NET5.COM.

A universal version of this file is also available. NETX.COM (note the capital X) works with all versions of DOS, but requires more memory than the various versions of NETx.COM.

Two variations of NETx.COM reduce the amount of DOS memory required to run the Network shell: one for running the shell in extended memory and another for running it in expanded memory.

- Extended memory is available on microcomputers equipped with 80286, 80386, or 80486 micro-processors and more than one megabyte (1024K) of memory. A memory driver such as HIMEM.SYS, which is provided with MS-DOS 5.0, must be loaded to support extended memory.

- Expanded memory is a special category of additional memory commonly referred to as LIM/EMS (Lotus/Intel/Microsoft Expanded Memory Specifications). LIM version 4.0 is required by NetWare.

    8088, 8086, and 80286 PCs require an add-in expanded memory board such as the Intel Above Board. 80386 and 80486 microcomputers that have more than one megabyte (1024K) of extended memory can use an EMS software driver to support expanded memory. MS-DOS Version 5.0 includes an EMS driver named EMM386.EXE for use on 386-based PCs, and third-party EMS drivers are available for earlier versions of DOS.

SHELL.CFG

SHELL.CFG is an optional file that is placed in the same workstation directory as IPX.COM and NETx.COM. It is a text file that contains commands that modify characteristics of the workstation's NetWare communication environment. A wide variety of commands are available for use in SHELL.CFG, some of which are presented in the tasks section.

Tasks

Configuring IPX.COM

Purpose

Use the WSGEN utility to create a version of IPX.COM that is configured for a particular brand of network interface card. WSGEN *links* IPX to an interface card configuration file.

Steps

1. Insert a copy of the WSGEN diskette in a drive. These steps assume that you are using A:.

2. Switch to the drive. Type **A:**.

3. Start WSGEN by entering **WSGEN**.

4. Press Enter to bypass the startup screen.

5. Scroll through the available network cards. If your card does not appear in the list, press Ins and follow the on-screen instructions to retrieve the configuration from your LAN_DRV_??? diskette.

6. Highlight the desired card and press Enter.

7. If a list of configuration options is presented, consult the card configuration data you collected before starting WSGEN. Select the required configuration option and press Enter.

   If the configuration of your card is not covered by one of the options, you must reconfigure your card.

8. Press Enter to configure IPX.COM.

   When WSGEN exits, the IPX.COM file on the diskette is configured for the target card. Copy this file to the workstation.

Notes

Several configuration files are shipped with WSGEN, but most network card manufacturers provide NetWare configuration files for their cards. If a disk accompanied your network card, it probably contained the configuration files. Two files are required, one each with the extension .LAN and the other the extension .OBJ.

If your WSGEN diskette contains room, you can copy these files onto a duplicate of the diskette. You can remove drivers you don't need from the copy. Otherwise, additional files must be installed on a diskette that has a volume label such as LAN_DRV_001. You can replace 001 with another three-digit number. This diskette is referred to as a LAN_DRV_??? diskette by WSGEN. Consult your network card documents for instructions on locating the files and preparing the LAN_DRV_??? diskette.

Before you begin to configure IPX.COM, write down the hardware configuration settings for your card. Exact items differ, but the following settings are common:

- **Interrupt Setting**. This setting is a number from 2 through 15 expressed in decimal digits. Interrupt settings are usually set by jumpers or switches on the interface card. IBM PS/2s and other micro-channel PCs are configured using the Reference Diskette that accompanied the computer.

- **I/O Base Address**. This setting is a three-digit hexadecimal number, such as 2E0h or 360h. Don't worry about counting in hexadecimal; just be aware that these are numbers that can contain letters for digits. Your board manual usually provides pictorial representations of the jumpers or switches for the available addresses.

- **RAM Address**. This setting is a hexadecimal number, such as CC00h, D000h, or D800h.

- **DMA Channel**. The Direct Memory Access channel is often specified for high-performance cards. This setting is a digit in the range of 1 to 7.

Few cards specify all of these items. Some cards are self-configuring and none of the preceding data is required to configure these cards in WSGEN.

Installing Shell Files on the Workstation

Purpose

Each workstation must have a copy of the appropriate IPX.COM and NETx.COM files. Common practice is to place these files in the root directory of the boot volume. This book recommends, however, that all NetWare files on the workstation be assembled in a directory. The directory name \NETWORK is used in all examples.

Steps

1. Change to the workstation boot drive.

   For example, type **C:**.

2. Create the network directory by typing
   MD \NETWORK.

3. Insert the WSGEN diskette in a diskette drive.

   This examples assumes that drive to be drive A:.

4. Copy these network files:

   COPY A:IPX.COM \NETWORK

   COPY A:NET5.COM \NETWORK

   The appropriate version of NETx.COM (NET3.COM, NET4.COM, etc.) should be copied.

5. Change to the \NETWORK directory so that the network shell files can be tested. Type **CD \NETWORK.**

6. Type **IPX.**

   If IPX installs successfully, a display such as the following is presented:

   ```
   Novell IPX/SPX v3.02 Rev. A (901218)
   (C) Copyright 1985, 1990 Novell Inc.  All
   Rights Reserved.

   LAN Option: NetWare NE/2  v2.02EC (900718)
   Hardware Configuration: IRQ = 3, I/O Base =
   1000h, Boot Prom Segment = C800h
   ```

7. Type the same of your NETx.COM file.

   For example, type **NET5.**

   If NETx finds a server, it displays a message similar to this:

   ```
   NetWare V3.22 - Workstation Shell (910731)
   (C) Copyright 1991 Novell, Inc.  All Rights
   Reserved.

   Running on DOS V5.00

   Attached to server FS1
   12-10-91    3:44:50 pm
   ```

8. Change to the network login directory, which is usually mapped to F:. Enter **F:.**

9. To log in, enter **LOGIN.**

Logging in from Batch Files

Purpose

Few users want to type all of the commands in the previous task every time they want to connect to the LAN. This task enables you to create a batch file to simplify the process.

Steps

Create this batch file using a text editor. You can name this batch file LAN.BAT, and put it in a directory on the workstation's search path.

```
C:
CD \NETWORK
IPX
NET5
F:
CLS
LOGIN
```

Alternately, you may want to put these commands at the end of the workstation's AUTOEXEC.BAT file. Then the workstation connects and displays a LOGIN prompt every time the workstation boots. You can include PROMPT and PATH commands in the AUTOEXEC.BAT file. A simple AUTOEXEC.BAT file follows:

```
ECHO OFF
CLS
PROMPT $P$G
PATH C:\DOS
C:
CD \NETWORK
IPX
NET5
F:
CLS
LOGIN
```

Displaying the NETx Configuration

Purpose

This task enables you to determine the revision level of a workstation's NETx.COM file.

Steps

You can display the configuration of the workstation NETx file by using the I option. Here is a typical configuration report produced by NETx I:

```
NetWare V3.22 - Workstation Shell (910731)
(C) Copyright 1991 Novell, Inc.  All Rights
Reserved.
```

Displaying the IPX Configuration

Purpose

This task enables you to determine the revision level and configuration options of its IPX.COM file.

Steps

You can view the configuration of any IPX.COM file by typing IPX I. The I option displays information about the IPX file, but does not attempt to install IPX on the workstation. The following output is a typical display produced by IPX I:

```
Novell IPX/SPX v3.02 Rev. A (901218)
(C) Copyright 1985, 1990 Novell Inc.  All Rights
Reserved.

LAN Option: NetWare NE/2  v2.02EC (900718)
Hardware Configuration: Set According to Micro
Channel Configuration
```

Reconfiguring IPX

Purpose

As you configure IPX.COM for workstations, it may be necessary to try several configuration options before you find an option that does not conflict with other hardware or software in the PC. You do not have to use WSGEN to generate a new IPX.COM file. All possible configurations are stored in IPX.COM. A new configuration choice can be specified with the DCONFIG utility, which is located on the WSGEN diskette.

Steps

1. Place the WSGEN diskette into a disk drive.

   This example assumes that you will use the A: drive.

2. Enter **A:DCONFIG C:\NETWORK\IPX.COM.**

   DCONFIG reports the options for this IPX file:

   ```
   Shell Driver: NetWare Ethernet NE2000  V1.03EC
   (891227)
     Node address is determined automatically.
        0: IRQ = 3, I/O Base = 300h, no DMA or RAM
        1: IRQ = 2, I/O Base = 320h, no DMA or RAM
        2: IRQ = 4, I/O Base = 340h, no DMA or RAM
        3: IRQ = 5, I/O Base = 360h, no DMA or RAM
        4: IRQ = 2, I/O Base = 300h, no DMA or RAM
        5: IRQ = 3, I/O Base = 320h, no DMA or RAM
        6: IRQ = 5, I/O Base = 340h, no DMA or RAM
        7: IRQ = 4, I/O Base = 360h, no DMA or RAM
        8: IRQ = 4, I/O Base = 300h, no DMA or RAM
        9: IRQ = 5, I/O Base = 320h, no DMA or RAM
      *10: IRQ = 2, I/O Base = 340h, no DMA or RAM
       11: IRQ = 3, I/O Base = 360h, no DMA or RAM
   ```

   The (*) marks the current IPX.COM settings.

3. To change IPX.COM to option 1, enter the following:

   A:DCONFIG C:\NETWORK\IPX.COM SHELL:,1

   The configuration options are listed again, with the asterisk indicating the newly selected option.

Notes

You can load IPX with different settings by using the /O*n* parameter. For example, IPX /05 loads IPX with configuration option 5. Use this procedure for testing various configurations. Then use DCONFIG to finalize the preferred configuration.

Running the NetWare Shell in Extended Memory

Purpose

This task enables you to use XMSNETx.EXE as a network shell. This version of the shell frees 34K of DOS memory compared to NETx.COM.

Steps

1. Determine the location of HIMEM.SYS on your PC. When it installs MS-DOS 5.0, the SETUP program places HIMEM.SYS in the \DOS directory of the boot drive.

2. Edit CONFIG.SYS to add the following line:

   DEVICE=C:\DOS\HIMEM.SYS

   Adjust the path in the DEVICE command if your copy of HIMEM.SYS is located elsewhere.

3. Copy the appropriate XMSNETx.EXE program file from the WSGEN diskette to the directory containing your NetWare workstation programs.

   Examples in this book assume that these files are in a directory named \NETWORK on the C: drive.

4. Edit your network startup batch files so that XMSNETx.EXE is used as the NetWare shell rather than NETx.COM.

5. Reboot the PC to install the new system drivers.

6. Execute the batch file that installs IPX.COM and XMSNETx.EXE. A connection to a network server should be established.

Notes

The NETx program usually shares the same memory that DOS dedicates for running user programs. Only 640K of memory is available to DOS programs. This memory allotment has become an increasingly burdensome restriction in recent years as application programs have grown in size and as users have become dependent on "pop-up" programs, technically called terminate and stay resident (TSR) programs. TSRs are loaded prior to loading applications and remain in the computer sharing memory resources.

The NETx programs also are classified as TSRs. They remain in memory as active programs until they are removed (at which time the link to the server is lost) or the PC is rebooted. NETx.COM ordinarily ties up some conventional DOS memory; therefore, Novell provides a variant that runs in *extended memory*.

In PCs based on 80286, 80386, or 80486 microprocessors, memory above 1 megabyte (1,024K) is extended memory. However, this memory is inaccessible to DOS unless an extended memory driver is installed. One such driver is HIMEM.SYS, which is included with MS-DOS 5.0.

Running the NetWare Shell in Expanded Memory

Purpose

You can use expanded memory as another way to make memory available in addition to the 640K that DOS normally provides. Expanded memory can be implemented on most PCs. PCs with 8088, 8086, and 80286 processors require an add-in expanded memory board, such as the Intel Above Board. If you have such a board properly configured for your computer, simply substitute

EMSNETx.EXE for NETx.COM to load the shell in expanded memory.

80386 and 80486 computers generally use a software system driver to configure extended memory as expanded memory. MS-DOS 5.0 includes the EMM386.EXE program as an expanded memory driver. The following steps illustrate a simple setup procedure. Both the HIMEM and EMM386 drivers have additional options that you may need to use on your computer.

Steps

1. Determine the location of HIMEM.SYS and EMM386.EXE on your PC. After it installs MS-DOS 5.0, the SETUP program places these files in the \DOS directory of the boot drive.

2. Edit CONFIG.SYS to add the following line:

   DEVICE=C:\DOS\HIMEM.SYS

   DEVICE=C:\DOS\EMM386.EXE RAM

   Adjust the paths in the DEVICE commands if your device drivers are located elsewhere. HIMEM.SYS must be installed prior to EMM386.EXE.

3. Copy the appropriate EMSNETx.EXE program file from the WSGEN diskette to the directory containing your NetWare workstation programs. Examples in this book assume that these files are in a directory named \NETWORK on the C: drive.

4. Edit any batch files so that EMSNETx.EXE is used instead of NETx.COM as the NetWare shell.

5. Reboot the PC to install the new system drivers.

6. Execute your network startup batch file. You should establish a connection with a network server.

Memory Managers, TSRs, and the NetWare Shell

Memory managers and TSR (terminate and stay resident) programs are essential for optimizing the performance of DOS PCs. Unfortunately, the more you use such programs the more likely it is that you will experience program conflicts.

Consideration of the various available memory management programs is beyond the scope of this book. Be aware that incompatibilities exist between certain revisions of these programs and the IPX.COM and NETx.COM programs.

When you add memory managers, first make sure that your PC can access the network without the memory manager. Examine the memory manager documentation carefully to see whether it specifies particular revisions of the NetWare shell programs. Execute IPX I and NETx I (see the next two sections) to see whether the programs on your workstation are the proper revisions.

Although a utility that is incompatible with the latest releases of IPX and NETx is not an uncommon problem, generally you should keep your NetWare files as up-to-date as possible.

If you can communicate with the server without the memory manager, experiment with the memory manager and its various options. The best memory managers also tend to be the most complicated because they have more configuration options.

Even when the memory manager and the NetWare communication programs appear to be working properly, you may encounter problems with various applications (memory managers and NetWare communication programs) that are sensitive to revision levels of DOS.

You probably won't be the first person to encounter a particular problem. The vendors of most memory managers and applications have various problem scenarios on hand. They also are familiar with the detailed compatibility needs of their products and with the more obscure problems that users might experience. If reasonable efforts do not correct the problem, call technical support for your software products.

Checking Communications with COMCHECK

Purpose

This task enables you to test the communication between two workstations. On occasion you may experience difficulty making workstations on the LAN communicate successfully. Problems may exist with wiring, or it may be that a version of IPX.COM simply doesn't agree with a workstation. You don't need to start IPX and NETx on each workstation for every test. The NetWare COMCHECK utility, located on the WSGEN diskette, is a useful diagnostic tool.

Recall that the workstation has two layers of NetWare software: IPX/SPX (IPX.COM) and the network shell (NETx.COM). IPX actually performs the communication between stations, and communication can be tested at the IPX level without confusing the issue with network shells or programs that may contain their own problems.

Steps

1. Run IPX.COM on one workstation.

2. Insert the WSGEN diskette in a diskette drive. Switch to that drive, and type **COMCHECK**.

3. COMCHECK asks you to enter a **Unique User Identification**. Enter something to identify this workstation such as:

   `Mary's PC`

4. A box is displayed that contains information about the workstation.

5. Repeat steps 1 through 3 on another workstation on the same network.

6. Both stations should display the information box. If they are in communication, information about both stations appears on each screen to indicate that both workstations are communicating with the network.

Notes

A station running COMCHECK broadcasts periodic messages announcing its presence on the LAN. Any station also running COMCHECK can receive these messages, which inform the receiving station that the sender is alive. Figure 3.1 illustrates a COMCHECK display with two PCs in conversation.

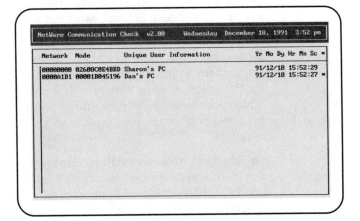

Figure 3.1: COMCHECK displaying two workstations in communication.

If neither station reports the presence of the other, you can determine whether the network is experiencing a general failure. Try running COMCHECK on some other stations to see whether the problem is widespread. If other stations are communicating, you may find that only one PC is refusing to acknowledge the others. Check the hardware in that PC, including network interface cards and cables. Swap hardware components to see whether you can isolate the bad item.

While testing cabling or PC hardware you can leave COMCHECK running. Each PC running COMCHECK continues to announce itself. If your efforts correct the problem, the various workstations begin to indicate proper communication.

If no stations are communicating, there is a general failure of the network. Cabling is usually the first thing to examine in these situations. Are there breaks in the cable? Are all connectors properly installed and are all connectors connected?

Less likely causes of general failures can be electronic devices that have failed or are generating noise on the network so that communication is garbled. Try shutting everything down and bringing up small parts of the network. The bad device may advertise itself when it starts up. You can choose to break large networks into smaller networks to make it quicker to locate the hardware offender.

Be aware of the communication characteristics of your LAN. Arm yourself with a diagram of the physical configuration of your network. By knowing the way in which your network operates and by plotting problems on the network diagram, you usually can isolate a single point of failure.

On Ethernet LANs every station talks to every other station; therefore, a network card failure will probably affect only one PC (unless the card is generating noise that affects everyone on the network).

On a thin or thick Ethernet segment, if station A sees station B, but B does not see A, the network as a whole probably is functional. Try running COMCHECK on another workstation to confirm this. You probably will find that this third workstation communicates properly with one of the test workstations and not with the other. In this case, suspect the workstation: either the network card or the entire PC.

Because 10BaseT Ethernets wire each workstation into an electronic hub or concentrator, it is possible for one workstation to be down while the rest of the network is functional. A single workstation failure can be due to cabling, to a port on the hub, or to failure of the workstation itself. Groups of failures may indicate a bad hub or concentrator.

A Token Ring passes messages around a ring. If workstation A does not communicate with B, the network may have a fault between the transmit side of A and the receive side of B: a bad cable or connector, for example. Or it may be that A's transmitter or B's receiver has failed. Check the cabling and try replacing network cards in both PCs.

If a station on a Token Ring stops passing on any message, stations past it on the ring stop receiving. If you know the order in which the stations are connected on the ring, you may be able to isolate the problem by seeing which stations are failing to receive COMCHECK messages.

 You can run COMCHECK on a server simply by booting the server to DOS using a bootable floppy diskette. Don't forget to run IPX before COMCHECK.

Enlarging the DOS Environment

Purpose

When it sets up the environment, DOS usually allocates only 160 bytes of memory in DOS 3.2 through 4.0 and 256 bytes in DOS 5.0. This memory can be used up quickly, and you may find it necessary to instruct DOS to maintain a larger environment. If environment variables are not being created properly, or if you see the message Out of environment space, you must reconfigure DOS for a larger environment.

The environment size is determined when DOS loads the command shell, which is usually COMMAND.COM. A SHELL command in CONFIG.SYS can be used to configure a larger environment.

Steps

1. Determine the location of your DOS COMMAND.COM file. This file is usually in the root of the work-station boot drive. C:\ is assumed in this example.

2. Edit the CONFIG.SYS file to include the following line:

   `SHELL=C:\COMMAND.COM C:\ /E:512/P`

3. Reboot the PC to install the larger environment.

Notes

SHELL loads and configures a DOS command shell. In addition to the shell command file, the following switches are used in this example.

- The value after /E: determines the environment size. You can vary the number after /E between 160 and 32,768.

- The /P switch makes the command shell permanent.

Increasing Network File Handles

Purpose

The FILES= statement in CONFIG.SYS determines how many DOS files the workstation can have open. This statement does not address the number of open server files, however.

NetWare users are normally given 40 *file handles* for opening files. If you receive the message no available files, your NetWare shell must be reconfigured to increase your file handles. This task teaches you the way in which you can increase available file handles.

Steps

1. Create or edit a file named SHELL.CFG. Place this file in the same directory with your IPX.COM and NETx.COM files. Examples in this book assume that these files are in the C:\NETWORK directory.

2. Add the following line to SHELL.CFG:

   FILE HANDLES=*n*

   where *n* represents the number of open files that are required. If your software documentation does not specify a number of file handles, increase this number gradually to eliminate the problem. Remember that file handles use up PC memory, so use only as many as are required.

3. Reboot the PC and log in to install the new option.

Specifying a Preferred Server

Purpose

On networks that have several servers, users must know how to connect with the servers they particularly need. When NETx.COM is run, it simply connects to the first server to respond to its connection request. If this is not the desired server, the user must know how to log in to the preferred one by including the server name before the login name.

If a PREFERRED SERVER command is placed in the user's SHELL.CFG command, the user is connected to the desired server.

Steps

1. Create or edit the SHELL.CFG file. Place this file in the same directory with your IPX.COM and NETx.COM files. Examples in this book assume that these files are in the C:\NETWORK directory.

2. Add the following line to SHELL.CFG:

   PREFERRED SERVER=*name*

   where *name* represents the name of the desired server.

3. Reboot the PC and log in to install the new option. After NETx.COM is executed, it should report that a connection has been established with the desired server.

Creating a Boot Diskette

Purpose

Boot diskettes are required for workstations that do not have hard drives, but they are handy to have for other workstations in case the local hard drive fails.

A task in the next chapter illustrates the way in which DOS program files can be installed on the server so that they can be readily accessed by PCs that boot from diskettes. This technique works only when the version of DOS on the server exactly matches the version used to boot the PC. To simplify things, therefore, it is advisable to create all boot diskettes from the same version of DOS. MS-DOS 5.0 is highly recommended as a standard.

Steps

1. Identify a PC that has the preferred version of DOS installed on the hard drive.

2. Insert a diskette in a disk drive. High-density diskettes (5 1/4-inch 1.2M or 3 1/2-inch 1.44M) are preferred so that there is plenty of space for drivers and network files.

3. Format the diskette and install the DOS system:

   FORMAT A: /S

   Substitute B: for A: if you are formatting a diskette in your second disk drive.

4. Type **DIR A:** and verify that COMMAND.COM is installed on the floppy diskette. If not, you must copy it from your hard drive.

5. Boot your PC with this new diskette to ensure that the system was properly installed.

6. Create the following CONFIG.SYS file on the diskette:

   ```
   FILES=20
   BUFFERS=1
   SHELL=COMMAND.COM  /E:512/P
   ```

7. Create this AUTOEXEC.BAT file on the diskette:

   ```
   PROMPT $P$G
   IPX
   NET5
   F:
   CLS
   LOGIN
   ```

8. Copy the following files to the floppy diskette:

   IPX.COM

   NETx.COM

9. If your network has more than one server, create a SHELL.CFG file on the diskette that has the following command:

   PREFERRED SERVER=name

   Substitute your server name for *name*.

Notes

You may need to add a line to SHELL.CFG to define a LONG MACHINE TYPE. Read Chapter 4: "Installing DOS Files on the Server" to see whether you should add this line before you do the installation.

4

CONFIGURATION

Network adminstrators invest considerable effort in configuring the server. A properly configured server is easier to maintain and provides a productive environment for users, one that it is little more complicated to use than a stand-alone PC.

In this chapter, you learn how to accomplish the following tasks:

- Install DOS files on the fileserver
- Create login scripts
- Use login script and DOS variables
- Understand NetWare menu basics

Key Concepts

After users log in to a NetWare server, one or more *login scripts* usually are executed. Login scripts contain commands that are executed every time a user successfully logs in to the server. The login script may perform some of the following functions:

- Setting up an initial set of drive maps and search drives

- Displaying important messages to users

- Connecting users to copies of DOS that are installed on the server

- Connecting users to network printers

- Starting a standard menu

Login scripts can be of several types. After NetWare is installed on a server, a *default login script* is established, which performs the most basic setup tasks. Unless the system administrator sets up user login scripts, the default script executes. The *system login script* is set up by the system administrator. It contains commands that execute after a user logs in. Each user can have a *personal login script* that contains commands that execute only when that user logs in.

Tasks

Installing DOS Files on the Server

Purpose

An advantage of connecting a PC to a LAN server is that the PC does not require its own hard disk. When workstations boot from floppy diskettes, however, they do not have enough disk space to store complete copies of DOS. Instead, the network server must be configured so that an appropriate copy of DOS is available to the workstation after network login is complete.

Workstations equipped with hard drives often benefit if they use the server-based copy of DOS. When DOS is upgraded, it is simpler to update the single copy on the server than it is to upgrade each PC individually.

This task is complicated because so many versions of DOS exist. The version of DOS on the LAN must exactly match the version that was used to place the system files on the diskette that is booted on the workstation. If possible, standardize all workstations on a single version of DOS, preferably MS-DOS 5.0. If you can't standardize, however, the next task shows you the way to install multiple versions of DOS, and connect each workstation with its required version.

Steps

1. Install MS-DOS 5.0 on a workstation.

2. Log in as the system supervisor from the DOS 5.0 workstation.

3. Create the directory to receive the DOS files by entering the following commands:

   `MD \PUBLIC\IBM_PC`

   `MD \PUBLIC\IBM_PC\MSDOS`

   `MD \PUBLIC\IBM_PC\MSDOS\V5.00`

4. Copy the files with this command:

   `NCOPY C:\DOS\*.* SYS:PUBLIC\IBM_PC\MSDOS\V5.00`

   The number of files copied is displayed.

5. Flag the DOS files as Shareable Read-Only. Enter the following command:

   `FLAG SYS:PUBLIC\IBM_PC\MSDOS\V5.00 SRO`

   A list of files with their attributes set to Ro (read-only) and S (shareable) is displayed.

6. Log out.

7. Log in.

8. Enter **MAP** and examine the search drive listings. You should see an entry similar to the following:

```
SEARCH2:  = Y:.  [FS1\SYS:   \PUBLIC\IBM_PC\MSDOS\V5.00]
```

Notes

If you have not defined user login scripts, Netware executes a default login script as each user logs in. The default script attempts to map search drive S2: to a DOS subdirectory, which should be set up like the preceding example.

If you do not see a DOS drive mapping, the default login script was replaced by login scripts that do not contain an appropriate MAP command. If you use user login scripts, the default login script does not run, and you must include commands in the system login script to map the user to the appropriate DOS directory. See "Configuring the System Login Script" for more information on making the required modifications.

DOS expects to find a file named COMMAND.COM on the drive from which the PC was booted. This requirement can present problems if a PC is booted from a diskette. If the diskette is removed, the file becomes unavailable. Users then receive the message Insert disk with COMMAND.COM. See "Changing the Location of COMMAND.COM" for a strategy that alleviates this problem.

Installing Additional Brands and Versions of DOS

Purpose

This task enables you to place different versions of DOS on the fileserver, even if they share the same version number. Once configured, each workstation maps the appropriate version of DOS. Suppose that your network configuration contains both Compaq computers and other IBM-compatible computers, and that you want to run the Compaq computers with Compaq MS-DOS. Two DOS versions must be installed on the fileserver in such a way that they can be accessed by the appropriate PCs.

Steps

This task assumes that MS-DOS 5.0 was installed according to the instructions in the previous task. In this task, install Compaq MS-DOS as follows:

1. Install Compaq MS-DOS 5.0 on a workstation.

2. Log in as the system supervisor from the Compaq workstation.

3. Create the directory to receive the DOS files by entering the following commands:

   `MD \PUBLIC\COMPAQ`

   `MD \PUBLIC\COMPAQ\MSDOS`

   `MD \PUBLIC\COMPAQ\MSDOS\V5.00`

4. Copy the files with this command:

   `NCOPY C:\DOS\*.* SYS:PUBLIC\COMPAQ\MSDOS\V5.00`

   The number of files copied is displayed by the system.

5. Flag the DOS files as Shareable Read Only. Enter

   `FLAG SYS:PUBLIC\COMPAQ\MSDOS\V5.00 SRO`

   A list of files with their attributes set to Ro (read-only) and S (shareable) is displayed.

6. Create or edit a SHELL.CFG file in the workstation directory used to load the NetWare IPX and NETx shells. See Chapter 3 for discussions about the SHELL.CFG file. Make sure that the SHELL.CFG file contains the following line:

   `LONG MACHINE TYPE=COMPAQ`

7. Log out and reboot.

8. Log in, being sure to execute IPX and NETx from the directory containing SHELL.CFG.

9. Change to drive F:.

10. Log in.

The correct version of DOS is mapped to drive Y:(search drive 2). The drive map looks like this:

```
SEARCH2:  = Y:. [DEVEL\SYS:\PUBLIC\COMPAQ\MSDOS\V5.00]
```

Notes

You can install more versions of DOS. Just remember to create a new LONG MACHINE TYPE for each version and to name the DOS directories accordingly.

The default LONG MACHINE TYPE is IBM_PC, even for workstations that were not manufactured by IBM. If you want to use IBM_PC exclusively for IBM brand workstations and PC-DOS, you must make sure that non-IBM PCs have a SHELL.CFG file with a different LONG MACHINE TYPE entry.

Creating the System Login Script

Purpose

Although Netware provides a default login script, you probably will want to enter a customized system login script and possibly user login scripts. Because the default login script does not run if you include a user login script, you should add several of the default commands to the system login script. This task shows the way in which to edit the system login script and makes some recommendations about the commands that should appear in it.

Steps

1. Log in as a system supervisor.

2. At the DOS prompt, enter **SYSCON**.

The SYSCON **Available Topics** menu is displayed.

3. Select **Supervisor Options**.

4. Select **System Login Script**.

   The current system login script is displayed.

5. Edit the system login script so that it contains the following commands:

```
MAP DISPLAY OFF
MAP ERRORS OFF
*** Map the public and DOS search drives
MAP INSERT S1:=SYS:PUBLIC
MAP INSERT S2:=SYS:PUBLIC\%MACHINE\%OS\%OS_VERSION
*** Map the home directories
MAP ROOT H:=SYS:HOME\%LOGIN_NAME
IF LOGIN_NAME="SUPERVISOR" THEN MAP H:=SYS:SYSTEM
MAP DISPLAY ON
WRITE "Good %GREETING_TIME, %LOGIN_NAME"
MAP
EXIT
```

6. Press Esc to save the newly edited system login script. The **Save Changes** menu is displayed.

7. Select **Yes** to save the new version of the system login script.

8. Quit SYSCON.

9. Log out.

10. Log in. The system now runs your new login script. Examine the MAP display. Then read the Notes for a description of the commands in the login script.

Tips on Editing Login Scripts

Use the cursor movement keys, the Delete, or Backspace keys to edit the login script. Press Enter in a line to break the line at the cursor. Press Enter at the end of a line to create a blank line.

The script editor contains no overtype mode. You always type in insert mode. You must delete unwanted text. The editor enables you to work with blocks of text in the following ways:

- To select a block of text, move the cursor to one end of the block and press F5. Then move the cursor to the other end of the block.

- After you select a block of text, delete it by pressing Del.

- After you delete a block of text, you can insert the block at another location. Move the cursor to the desired spot and press Ins.

- Press Ins several times to create multiple copies of a text block.

The login script is stored in the file `SYS:PUBLIC\NET$LOG.DAT`. This text file can be edited with a text editor. You may want to use another editor with more advanced features to make major changes. You must flag `NET$LOG.DAT` as Read Write before you can save a replacement version.

Notes

The following lines in the sample login script prevent the display of map activity that is of little interest to the user:

```
MAP DISPLAY OFF

MAP ERRORS OFF
```

NetWare does not echo each drive map as it is created. Nor does it warn of each error when a map fails. An error occurs when the supervisor logs in because an attempt is made to map `H:` to `SYS:HOME\SUPERVISOR`, a non-existent directory. Another error occurs if an attempt is made to map a DOS search drive when the proper version of DOS is not installed on the server.

The next two lines create basic network search drives for the `PUBLIC` and `DOS` directories. The second line uses several login script variables to determine the version of DOS that is running on the user's workstation. These variables are described in a later task.

```
MAP INSERT S1:=SYS:PUBLIC

MAP INSERT S2:=SYS:PUBLIC\%MACHINE\%OS\%OS_VERSION
```

Notice the use of INSERT in the MAP command. When a user first logs in, the drives in the workstation's PATH statement automatically map to search drives starting with S1:. MAP INSERT inserts maps for the PUBLIC and DOS directories, pushing the user's path directories up to start at S3:, which permits the user to retain search drive capability to directories on a local drive. By inserting the network directories as the first two search drives, you are assured that users will access commands in the PUBLIC and DOS directories before accessing commands on their local drives.

Remember that search drive letters are inserted into the user's DOS PATH environment variable. When the user logs out of the network, the network drives are removed from the path, which then returns to its prelogin state.

If the MAP command did not use INSERT, the PUBLIC and DOS directories overwrite the first two directories that appear in the user's original PATH statement. With each login/logout cycle, entries are lost in the user's environment PATH variable.

 If the DOS version on the user's workstation does not exactly match the specifications of one of the DOS versions installed on the server, the MAP INSERT for S2: does not take place. Unless the user had a DOS directory in the workstation PATH, the user cannot search for DOS commands.

Items following the percent sign (%) in the second MAP command are NetWare login variables. These variables are configured by NetWare to reflect the version of DOS that was used to boot the PC. Login variables are discussed in greater detail later in this chapter.

These lines are responsible for mapping HOME directories:

```
MAP ROOT H:=SYS:HOME\%LOGIN_NAME

IF LOGIN_NAME="SUPERVISOR" THEN MAP H:=SYS:SYSTEM
```

These lines also use login script variables to determine the user's login ID. The H: drive for user DSMITH is mapped to SYS:HOME\DSMITH. The SUPERVISOR does not have a home directory; therefore, an IF statement makes an exception for that ID and maps H: to SYS:SYSTEM. A later task discusses IF statements in login scripts.

This line displays a personalized user greeting:

```
WRITE "Good %GREETING_TIME, %LOGIN_NAME"
```

Next the login script displays the current drive mappings with a MAP command.

Finally, the login script includes an EXIT command. When this command appears in a system login script, NetWare quits the login script and displays a command prompt. Because NetWare has exited the login script, neither the default nor the user's personal login script is executed. If you do not plan to have a personal login script for every user, you should include an EXIT command as the last line of the system login script.

If a user does not have a user login script, the default login script executes after the system login script. Some commands in the default login script may modify the results of the system login script. The default login script also maps search drives to PUBLIC and DOS directories; therefore, two PUBLIC and DOS search maps are established. Avoid using the default login script once a system login script is set up.

To prevent execution of the default login script, follow one of these procedures:

- Make sure that the users' login scripts are not empty. You can, for example, include the statement MAP DISPLAY OFF. Any command in the user login script, even a REM, prevents the default login script from running.

- Add an EXIT to the end of the system login script. When EXIT is present, neither the default login script nor any user login scripts are executed. Include the command PCCOMPATIBLE in the login script before EXIT to ensure that all PCs can run EXIT correctly.

If a program should be run for all users at the end of the login script, EXIT can be followed by a 14-character command. This command appears in quotation marks after EXIT. For example, To execute the Novell menu program with a menu named MNU1, put the following command at the end of your system login script:

```
EXIT "MENU MNU1"
```

Comments in login scripts are extremely valuable. A comment is a line in the script that explains the action of the login script. NetWare ignores comments. A comment begins with REM, a semicolon (;), or an asterisk (*).

 Use comments to deactivate a command without removing it from the login script. The following comment line displays a login message if the asterisk is removed:

```
*FDISPLAY SYS:PUBLIC\NEWS.TXT
```

Creating User Login Scripts

Purpose

This task enables you to create a specific user login script, even if it only contains a remark, for a user who does not encounter an EXIT command in the system login script.

Steps

1. Log in as the supervisor or as the user you want to modify.

2. From the DOS prompt, enter **SYSCON**.

3. From the **Available Topics** menu, select **User Information**.

4. From the **User Names** menu, select the user to be modified.

5. From the **User Information** menu, select **Login Script**.

6. A box prompts you with **Read Login Script from User** followed by the user name. To modify the user's script, press Enter. Press Ins to select another user whose login script you want to use as a pattern.

7. Edit the user login script as required.

8. Press Esc. Quit SYSCON if desired.

Notes

Enter individual login commands in the user login script. To include personal drive maps or select the default printer the user wants to use, for example, enter the commands in the user login script.

Using Login Script Variables

Purpose

This task describes several login variables and explains the way in which they can be used in login script commands. A *variable* is a name that a computer program gives to data. A variable resembles a blank on a form, which can be filled in with any valid information. When a user logs in, NetWare fills in several variables with information about the user, the user's PC, the date and time, and so forth. This information can be retrieved while the commands in the login scripts are executed.

Steps

To retrieve the value of a login variable, include the variable name in a login script command. If the variable name appears in place of explicit text, a percent sign (%) must precede the variable. The percent sign indicates to NetWare that the value of the variable is to be substituted. Without the percent sign, NetWare simply uses the variable name itself.

Notes

The basic system login script in the previous task made use of several NetWare login variables. Three appear in this line alone:

```
MAP INSERT
S2:=SYS:PUBLIC\%MACHINE\%OS\%OS_VERSION
```

This command contains the following login variables:

- `MACHINE` has a value defined by the `LONG MACHINE TYPE` line in the PC's `SHELL.CFG` file. If this line is not found in `SHELL.CFG`, NetWare sets the value of `MACHINE` to `IBM_PC`.

- `OS` stores the name of the operating system, usually MS-DOS.

- `OS_VERSION` contains the DOS version number that was used to boot the workstation.

If these variables appear in a login script, NetWare substitutes the text represented by the variable into the command.

Table 4.1 lists the most useful Netware variables.

Table 4.1
Useful NetWare Login Variables

Login variables	Explanation
DAY	Day number (01-31)
DAY_OF_WEEK	Sunday through Saturday
MONTH	Month number (01-12)
MONTH_NAME	January through December
NDAY_OF_WEEK	Weekday number (1-7, Sunday=1)
SHORT_YEAR	Year in short format (91, 92, 93)
YEAR	Year in full format, such as 1992

Login variables	Explanation
HOUR	Hour (1-12)
HOUR24	Hour (00-23)
MINUTE	Minute (00-59)
SECOND	Second (00-59)
AM_PM	Day or night (am or pm)
GREETING_TIME	Morning, afternoon or evening
NETWORK_ADDRESS	Network number of PC (8 hex digits)
P_STATION	PC node address (12 hex digits)
FULL_NAME	User's full name
LOGIN_NAME	User's login name
USER_ID	Number assigned to each user
MEMBER OF *"group"*	TRUE if user is member of the group, otherwise false.

The example system login script contains several commands that use login variables. Often login variables are used simply to display information, as in this example:

```
WRITE "Good %GREETING_TIME, %LOGIN_NAME"
```

Login variables can be put to more complex use, however. In this command, the LOGIN_NAME variable retrieves the user's login name so that the user's H: drive is mapped to his personal home directory:

```
MAP H:=SYS:HOME\%LOGIN_NAME
```

For user DSMITH, this command is equivalent to the following:

```
MAP H:=SYS:HOME\DSMITH
```

The login variable makes it possible to adapt the command to each user.

Using IF in Login Scripts

Purpose

Use the IF command to execute commands only if certain conditions apply. Here are some instances that call for use of IF:

- Members of the group ACCT should have drive J: mapped to SYS:ACCT.

- Users who log in on a particular network segment should be warned that maintenance is scheduled for 5:00 P.M.

- A message should be displayed only if it is Friday, and the user is a member of the SALES group.

Steps

After IF, include the *conditions* that determine whether the command should be carried out. Follow the conditions with the command to be executed.

Here is a simple IF statement that prints a message on Friday only:

```
IF DAY_OF_WEEK="Friday" THEN WRITE "Don't forget your time sheet!"
```

Notes

If a variable appears as part of the condition of an IF statement, do not precede the variable with a percent sign.

In the previous example, DAY_OF_WEEK was examined to see if its value was the word Friday, which is an example of a *string*. In computers, a string is any series of text characters that is to be treated literally. Strings are presented inside quotation marks to distinguish them from commands and variables.

The case of the characters is important to NetWare. "Friday" is not "friday," for example. If the command reference lists the possible values for a NetWare login variable, you must adhere to the case of the letters.

The conditional part of an IF statement usually consists of three parts:

- A variable that is to be tested

- The test to be applied

- A value, usually a string, against which the variable is to be tested

Many variations on the conditions of variables and IF statements can exist. Equality and inequality tests even provide further operators. These operators include:

- Test equality with =, ==, IS, or EQUALS.

- Test inequality with !=, <>, IS NOT, DOES NOT EQUAL, or NOT EQUAL TO.

- Use the NOT operator to reverse the effect of any test.

- You can test for Greater Than (>), Less Than (<), Greater Than or Equal To (>=), and Less Than or Equal To (<=).

- Use AND and OR to combine the results of several tests.

Here is an example of an inequality:

```
IF DAY_OF_WEEK!="Friday" THEN WRITE "Have a nice day!"
```

This message displays on any day but Friday. If you want to have one message displayed Monday through Thursday and another message on Friday, you could use the two IF statements represented so far.

This either/or situation is so common, however, that an ELSE clause can be added to an IF statement:

```
IF DAY_OF_WEEK="Friday" THEN
WRITE "Don't forget your time sheet!"
ELSE
WRITE "Have a nice day!"
END
```

The commands following THEN are executed if the condition is true. The commands following ELSE are executed if the condition is false.

Notice the END keyword after the ELSE clause. END is optional in simple IF...THEN statements, but is required when an ELSE clause is added.

Inequalities can be used to see whether a value falls within a specified range. To remind members of the sales staff that expense reports are due by the seventh day of each month, the following IF statement can be used:

```
IF VALUE DAY < "7" THEN
WRITE "Remember: Sales reports are due by the
7th!"
END
```

The VALUE keyword informs NetWare to perform the tests by using numeric values, not the characters that represent the number. Computers represent numbers differently from strings, and the number 5 is different from the string "5".

Character comparisons are performed alphabetically according to a character coding system called ASCII. If VALUE is missing, DAY is less than "7" on the 15th of the month because "1" is alphabetized before "7" in ASCII.

The last example sends the message to everyone on the LAN, not just to the sales staff. The AND operator allows several conditions to be combined. Consider this example:

```
IF VALUE DAY < "7" AND MEMBER OF "SALES" THEN
WRITE "Remember: Sales reports are due by the 7th!"
END
```

AND and OR combine the results of several tests. AND is true if both of its tests are true. OR is true if either test is true.

The last example introduced the MEMBER OF login variable, which is unique because it does not represent a fixed value. Instead, it performs a test and has the value of TRUE if the test succeeds and FALSE if the test fails. Thus, if DSMITH logs in and is a member of the ACCT group, his J: drive is mapped as specified.

Using MEMBER OF with groups is a powerful way of performing tasks selectively for different users. Here are some possibilities:

- Connect users in departments to their preferred printers (See Chapter 6).

- Map a shared directory for each department to contain common files such as spreadsheets or databases.

- Present meeting reminders, department news, or calendar events to specific users.

Comparisons can be made alphabetically. Here is an involved example:

```
IF FULL_NAME <= "G" AND DAY_OF_WEEK = "Tuesday" THEN WRITE

"Please attend benefits orientation today at 3:00."<Enter>

IF FULL_NAME >= "H" AND FULL_NAME <= "N" AND DAY_OF_WEEK
="Wednesday" THEN WRITE "Please attend benefits orientation

today at 3:00."<Enter>

IF FULL_NAME > "N" AND DAY_OF_WEEK = "Thursday" THEN WRITE

"Please attend benefits orientation today at 3:00."<Enter>
```

If several comparisons are made, the IF statements can exceed a line in length. As you type these statements, allow the lines to continue on succeeding lines. Don't press Enter until the end of the last line of the statement. In the preceding example, <Enter> shows where the Enter key was pressed.

VALUE does not appear; therefore, these comparisons are made alphabetically. Chapter 2 recommended that Users be given full names in a "Last Name, First Name" format. This example shows the usefulness of that approach. Users are broken into three groups by the alphabetical position of their last names.

Until now the examples have included only one command after THEN. When more than one command must be executed as a result of a condition, the commands must be placed in a block, beginning with BEGIN and ending with either ELSE or END. Consider this example:

```
IF MEMBER OF "SALES" THEN BEGIN

MAP J:=SYS:SALES

WRITE "Sales reports are due by the 7th!"

END
```

An ELSE clause can be added like this:

```
IF MEMBER OF "SALES" THEN BEGIN

MAP J:=SYS:SALES

WRITE "Sales reports are due by the 7th!"

ELSE

MAP J:=SYS:COMMON

END
```

Using DOS Variables in Login Scripts

Purpose

Use DOS environment variables to communicate between DOS and login scripts.

Steps

1. Assign the information to a DOS variable before you log in.

2. Log in to the server.

3. Reference the DOS variable between angle braces (< and >) in the login script.

Notes

As an illustration, this technique will be used to solve a common problem experienced by users who boot from floppy diskettes. Recall that these users must be careful not to remove the boot floppy because DOS looks for COMMAND.COM on that disk.

The location of COMMAND.COM is stored in the environment variable COMSPEC. Your login script can retrieve COMSPEC and see whether COMMAND.COM is on the A: drive. If so, COMSPEC can be changed to point to the copy of DOS that the workstation is using on the server.

If your workstation boots from a diskette, SET normally shows the following information for the environment variable COMSPEC:

```
COMSPEC=A:\COMMAND.COM
```

To make this PC work better with the copy of DOS on the server, if Y: is mapped to a copy of DOS, it is preferable to change the COMSPEC value to

```
COMSPEC=Y:\COMMAND.COM
```

The following command, if placed after the MAP INSERT S2: statement in the example login script, modifies COMSPEC for users booting from A: drives:

```
IF <COMSPEC>="A:\COMMAND.COM" THEN
COMSPEC=S2:\COMMAND.COM
```

Because the sample login script maps S2: to the DOS drive (the drive letter for which is normally Y:), this command has the desired result of setting COMSPEC to the server DOS directory.

Using Login Script Variables in DOS

Purpose

Often, NetWare login script variables contain information that is useful in DOS commands. You can use this technique, for example, to have a batch file map to a directory name that is based on the user's login name.

Steps

To communicate information between the login script and DOS, use the DOS SET command.

The following line in a login script stores a string value in a DOS variable:

```
DOS SET DEPT="ACCT"
```

More commonly, however, you will want to capture the value of a login script variable. This example stores the user's login name in a DOS variable:

```
DOS SET USERID="%LOGIN_NAME"
```

Notes

The value to the right of the equal sign is always enclosed in quotation marks. The percent sign identifies the text inside the quotation marks as a variable.

Remember that the size of the user's environment is determined when the workstation boots DOS. Be sure the environment is large enough to contain the values you want to assign. Use the techniques presented in Chapter 3 to enlarge the environment.

The value of this technique is limited only by your imagination.

Consider as an example the need for some applications to be started with a configuration that corresponds to the video card in the workstation. If the batch file lists workstations by network address along with their corresponding video cards, it can select the appropriate startup commands.

The following line in a login script stores the workstation's network address in a variable named PST:

```
DOS SET PST="%NETWORK_ADDRESS"
```

The following batch file can take advantage of this information:

```
IF "%PST%"=="0000D03E123A" GOTO MONO
IF "%PST%"=="000000000015" GOTO CGA
IF "%PST%"=="0000D03F245C" GOTO VGA
ECHO Cannot start application. PST variable is missing.
ECHO Consult the LAN administrator.
GOTO EXIT
:VGA
REM include commands for use with a VGA monitor
GOTO EXIT
```

```
:CGA
REM include commands for use with a CGA monitor
GOTO EXIT
:MONO
REM include commands for use with a MONO monitor
:EXIT
```

In the batch file, quotation marks are placed around the variable names and the network addresses in the IF statements. When an IF statement in a batch file tries to compare two values, an error results if one of the values is empty. By placing quotation marks around the variable name, IF sees something to compare even when the variable is empty. IF PST has no value, the first comparison results in an error since DOS would interpret it as

IF =="0000D03E123A" GOTO MONO

In the example batch file, a message is displayed if PST has not been assigned a value. It is a good idea to include error messages such as this in your batch files.

Using NetWare Menus

Purpose

A carefully configured network server rarely confronts users with network issues. Users do not need to know how to map drives or where their command files are found.

A well-designed menu *is* the network for most users. Users can remain oblivious to the source of a computer resource, whether it is coming from the local PC or from the server.

This task illustrates a simple menu that uses the NetWare menu utility. This menu can be easily extended to incorporate additional applications and features.

Steps

1. Log in as a supervisor.

2. Create the following menu directory:

   MD F:\MENU

3. As users use the menu, temporary files are created. Users must have the ability to create and erase files in the menu directory. Grant the necessary rights to group EVERYONE:

```
GRANT R W C E F IN SYS:MENU TO GROUP EVERYONE
```

4. Use a text editor to create the following file. Name it MENU01.MNU and store the file in SYS:MENU. If a line is indented below, be sure to indent it by at least two spaces when you create the file.

```
%Main Menu,8,15
A. Edit
  \@ECHO OFF
  MAP INSERT S1:=SYS:APPS\EDIT > NUL:
  MAP ROOT M:=H: > NUL:
  M:
  MD DOCS > NUL:
  CD DOCS > NUL:
  CLS
  ECHO Standby...Starting EDIT
  EDIT
  CLS
  ECHO Standby...Returning to menu
  F:
  MAP DEL S1: > NUL:
  MAP DEL M: > NUL:
X. Utilities
  %Utilities
Z. Logout
  F:
  !LOGOUT

%Utilities,12,40
Display file directory
  DIR @1"Source drive"@2"Directory path"\\@3"File
  specification"¦MORE
  PAUSE
Set Your Password
  SETPASS
  PAUSE
```

View NetWare Maps
  MAP
  PAUSE

> Be sure to type the DIR command line that follows
> Display file directory as a single long line.

5. Flag the menu file as Shareable Read Only. Since
   users have Erase privileges in this directory, they
   should be prevented from accidentally erasing the
   menu file.

   FLAG SYS:MENU*.MNU S RO

6. Use SYSCON to modify the system login script. It
   should be functionally equivalent to this:

```
MAP DISPLAY OFF
MAP ERRORS OFF
PCCOMPATIBLE
REM Map the public and DOS search drives
MAP INSERT S1:=SYS:PUBLIC
MAP INSERT S2:=SYS:PUBLIC\%MACHINE\%OS\%OS_VERSION
REM Map the home directories
MAP ROOT H:=SYS:HOME\%LOGIN_NAME
IF LOGIN_NAME="SUPERVISOR" THEN MAP H:=SYS:SYSTEM
WRITE "Good %GREETING_TIME, %LOGIN_NAME"
MAP F:=SYS:MENU
DRIVE F:
IF NOT MEMBER OF "NOMENU" THEN EXIT "MENU MENU01"
```

For purposes of this demonstration, also do the following:

1. Create the directory SYS:APPS\EDIT.

2. Grant group EVERYONE rights to the EDIT directory:

   GRANT R F IN SYS:APPS\EDIT TO GROUP EVERYONE

3. Copy EDIT.EXE from a copy of MS-DOS Version 5.0
   into SYS:APPS\EDIT.

When users log in to the server, the sample menu should be
presented as soon as login is completed. Log in and examine
the menu features before you read the "Notes" section.

First examine the last three lines of the login script:

- Drive F: is mapped to the menu directory. Any drive letter can be used; be sure to change the references to F: in the menu file, however.

- The DRIVE statement changes the working drive to F:. This ensures that menu temporary files will be created in the SYS:MENU directory.

- Finally, if a user is not a member of the NOMENU group, the MENU program is called and asked to run MENU01. Most users will not be in NOMENU and will receive the menu after login. Members of NOMENU will be sent on to their user login scripts. *Make sure that all members of NOMENU have personal login scripts.*

The following features are included in the MENU01 menu:

- Any line that is flush with the left margin and begins with a % is a menu title line. This menu contains two menu title lines:

```
%Main Menu,8,15

%Utilities,12,40
```

The numbers following the menu titles represent the row and column on the screen on which the center of the menu box is located. Generally, it is easiest to simply use trial and error to get menus positioned pleasingly. Leave these entries blank to center the menu box on the screen.

The first line of the file defines the first menu box that will be displayed.

- All other flush left lines are item titles. The titles within a given menu box are alphabetized when they are displayed. For this reason, the items in the Main menu start with a letter to control the order in which they are displayed. One approach is to alphabetize the most commonly-used utilities first. Remember that users get in the habit of typing certain keys for certain options; change the key letters as infrequently as possible.

- Any line that is indented and begins with a % displays a submenu with the specified name. A line like this appears in the main menu:

```
X. Utilities
   %Utilities
```

A matching menu must be defined somewhere else in the file. The submenu for this option starts with this line:

```
%Utilities,12,40
```

- Any command following an item title is executed when the item title is selected. These commands must be indented two or more spaces or they are interpreted as menu options.

Examine the commands for A. Edit carefully. They have the following features:

- An M: drive map is created that initially points to the user's home directory. After M: is selected, an attempt is made to create a DOCS subdirectory; then a CD command causes the system to change to that subdirectory. This ensures that all users start in a uniform directory.

- A search map is created in the menu and is inserted into S1: so that its location is known.

- Both the M: and S1: drive maps are deleted when the user exits the application. With only 26 letters available, drive maps are at a premium. By creating them as needed and deleting them when they are no longer required, you can avoid running out of letters.

- As many distracting messages as possible are suppressed so that the screens are more attractive. More importantly, however, it reduces the distraction to users who do not know or care how DOS works.

The first line turns DOS echo off.

Lines that end with > NUL: are using the DOS redirection operator to send any output from the command to a non-displaying device.

- ECHO is used to display messages to users when there may be a pause.

- The LOGOUT command is preceded with an exclamation point like this:

    !LOGOUT

    The exclamation point indicates that the menu program is to exit before running the command. If it doesn't, several error messages are displayed after the LOGOUT command executes. They result because the MENU program builds two temporary files in the menu directory. One is a batch file that is used by MENU to resume its operation after a command is executed. Without the !, MENU will attempt to resume after logging the user out of the server, but the batch files will be unavailable.

- If a command produces a display that a user needs time to examine, be sure to include a PAUSE command.

- The COPY option uses variables to collect user input. @1, @2, and @3 specify a message that is to be displayed and wait for user input. After the user has supplied answers to all three prompts, the answers are assembled along with the text in the menu command line to build a final command that is sent to DOS.

- The % and @ characters are special to the MENU program. If you want one of these characters to appear as text in a command line, you must precede it with a \ so that MENU knows it is to be treated as a plain text character. In the following line, \ must precede @ so that @ is considered part of the ECHO command:

    \@echo off

Because \ is used to mark special characters as text, it is also a special character. If you want a \ in a menu command, it must be entered twice, as in this line:

```
DIR @1"Source drive"@2"Directory path"\\@3"File
    specification"¦MORE
```

Displaying NetWare Menus on Monochrome Monitors

Purpose

By default, colors on NetWare menus are intended for display on color monitors. If a workstation is equipped with a monochrome monitor, menus may lack contrast and be hard to read. A simple change, however, can make the menus display in monochrome.

Steps

Create or modify an existing SHELL.CFG file on the user workstation. Be sure that this file is in the directory from which IPX.COM and NETx.COM are executed.

Include the following line in the SHELL.CFG file:

```
SHORT MACHINE TYPE=CMPQ
```

Notes

Netware uses a series of files in the SYS:PUBLIC directory to control menu colors (and other functions as well). Usually, NetWare uses the file IBM$RUN.OVL to control menu colors. NetWare also installs a file named CMPQ$RUN.OVL, however, which is configured for monochrome menus.

The file you use is determined by the value of SHORT MACHINE TYPE, which defaults to IBM. Therefore, the IBM$RUN.OVL file is usually used and menus are displayed in color. By changing this value to CMPQ in the SHELL.CFG file, the workstation accesses the CMPQ$RUN.OVL file.

You may need more menu color configurations. If so, examine the materials about the COLORPAL utility in the NetWare manuals.

Logging Out From a Batch File

Purpose

Batch files can make it easier to access network services. If a batch file is used to log out, however, it must be configured properly or users receive the message ?BATCH FILE NOT FOUND.

The trick is to make sure that the user can access the batch file even after the logout has taken place. Because users can execute files in SYS:LOGIN even though they are logged out (the LOGIN.EXE command file is located there, for example), this is a good place for logout batch files. SYS:LOGIN is not usually mapped to a search drive; therefore, two batch files may be required:

- The first batch file is located in a search directory such as SYS:PUBLIC. It changes the directory to SYS:LOGIN and starts the second batch file.

- The second batch file executes the final logout commands.

Steps

1. Log in as a supervisor.

2. Using a text editor, create a batch file named BYE.BAT. Store this file in SYS:PUBLIC or another directory that is mapped to a search drive for all users. BYE.BAT should contain the following commands:

```
REM SYS:PUBLIC\BIN\BYE.BAT
MAP F:=SYS:LOGIN
F:
LOGOUTIN
```

3. Create the following batch file, named LOGOUTIN.BAT and store it in SYS:LOGIN:

```
REM SYS:LOGIN\LOGOUTIN.BAT
NLOGOUT
CLS
LOGIN
```

When the user executes BYE, BYE.BAT switches to SYS:LOGIN and calls LOGOUTIN.BAT, which executes LOGOUT.EXE to log the user out, clears the screen, and then executes LOGIN. The user sees a clear screen containing the message Enter your login name:.

Changing the File Server Time and Date

Purpose

When IPX and NETx run on a workstation, that workstation's time and date are adjusted to match the server's date and time. If the clock in the server isn't correct, neither are the clocks in the workstations. This task teaches you to change the date and time in NetWare.

Steps

1. Log in as the supervisor.

2. At the DOS prompt, start **FCONSOLE**.

3. From the **Available Options** menu, select **Status**. The **File Server Status** panel is displayed.

4. Move to the **Server Date** field and enter a new date in the MM-DD-YYYY format.

   To enter October 15, 1992, for example, type **10-15-1992** and press Enter.

5. Move to the **Time** field and enter a new time in the hh:mm am or pm format,.

   To enter 4:59 p.m., for example, type **4:59 pm** and press Enter.

6. Press Esc to save the new date and time.

7. Quit FCONSOLE if desired.

   Users who log in synchronize their workstations to the new time and date.

Notes

Changing the file server date and time in this manner is noted in the accounting file. You can view the accounting file by changing to the \SYSTEM directory and typing **PAUDIT**.

Installing Application Software

Purpose

Many commercial applications are designed with networks in mind. Manuals for these programs describe approved methods for installation on a network server. You may want to run standard applications from a network server. Although properly installing all the application software available for NetWare servers is beyond the scope of this book, this task discusses important pointers to proper LAN software installation.

Steps

If your application software directly supports your version of NetWare, follow the instructions supplied with the application. Otherwise, follow these suggested steps.

1. Make a subdirectory to contain the software you want to install. Group applications together by placing applications on a separate volume, one named APPS, for example. Alternatively, you can create an APPS directory on SYS: and install each application in a subdirectory of APPS, in SYS:APPS/MYNEWAP, for example.

2. Start SYSCON and create a group with trustee rights to the subdirectory in which you installed the software. If more than one subdirectory is

involved, add them all to the group. In general, assign the fewest rights that are necessary to run the program.

3. In each application directory involved, use FLAG to set all .EXE, .COM, .BAT, and .OVL files as Shareable Read-Only (SRO) as in the following example:

```
FLAG *.COM SRO
FLAG *.BAT SRO
```

4. Create a batch file or menu option for your users that creates a drive map to the software. See the menu example earlier in this chapter for a basic set of commands.

5. If you want to run the program in a multiuser mode (even though it was intended for a single user), try the procedures in steps 6 through 9.

6. First, perform these simple tests:

   - Use FCONSOLE (Netware 2.x) or MONITOR (Netware 3.x) to view the open files for any user running the new application.

   - See whether any temporary work files are created. Note their names.

   - See whether any of the data files are opened for Read/Write access.

7. If no work files are opened, start the application, configure the application completely (this process modifies at least one data file), return to DOS, and FLAG all of the files in the directory SRO. You now can attempt to run the application from more than one workstation.

8. If the application does create temporary work files and their locations can be changed by setting an environment variable, set the variable to the home directory (usually something like SET TEMP=F:\USERS\%USERID%) and try to run the application from more than one workstation. %USERID% is a DOS variable that was created using the procedure described in the task "Using Login Script Variables in DOS" earlier in this chapter.

9. If the software application does not allow you to set an environment variable for the temporary work file location, try this:

```
...
REM Batch file segment to run new non-network
application
MAP INSERT S1:=SYS:APPS\NEWPROG
H:
NEWPROG.EXE
MAP DELETE S1:
F:
...
```

The software now runs from the user's home directory because the application executable files and data files are found on the s1: search drive automatically.

Notes

If you are using an application that does not recognize network printing, make sure that you enable a printer before you attempt printing on a LAN-based printer. If printing does not start until you exit the application, you can specify that if the server does not receive print output in a certain number of seconds, that the file is placed in the queue for printing. Place the number of seconds in your CAPTURE command. For example, if you type TIMEOUT=10, the system knows to wait 10 seconds after the last piece of data is sent to the print queue. See Chapter 5 for more information about printing in NetWare.

 Non-network applications can damage data files. Make sure that you perform a backup before you attempt to run non-network applications, especially in multiuser mode.

5

PRINTING

One reason organizations have networks is to facilitate sharing of printers among large numbers of users. Unless users have exclusive use of printers that are attached to their workstations, they use shared printers that are managed by NetWare.

In addition to saving printer costs, network printing has other advantages. Users can select from printers in various locations and departments, for example. Perhaps the greatest advantage, however, is that you can send a job to a network printer and quickly regain control of your workstation while the printing is managed by the network server.

This chapter discusses the following topics:

- Local and network printing
- Setting up print queues
- Configuring a print server
- Print servers and remote printers
- Sending print jobs to network printers
- Managing print queues
- Defining and using print job configurations

Key Concepts

If you print to a personal printer, a cable connects your PC to the printer. In addition to transmitting data to the printer, this cable communicates several signals between the printer and the PC. A signal on one wire in the cable may inform the PC that the printer is out of paper and that it cannot receive data at the moment. Because the printer and PC communicate directly with each other through a wire, they can make their requirements known quite directly.

A PC talks to a network printer through a more indirect and complicated method. First, the printer data must be diverted from the local printer port to the network interface card, which communicates with the server. The server receives the data to be printed and stores it in a file called a *queue*. Then the server attempts to route the data to the requested printer, which may be connected to an entirely different PC. Before the job actually starts to print, the original PC can send all its data and go to its next task.

This scenario is rather involved, and it is up to the system administrator to put together the pieces so that it can take place smoothly.

Network Print Queues

Print queues solve the same problems as queues at a theater box office. Patrons of a theater arrive at irregular intervals. When too many patrons arrive for the ticket seller to handle immediately, they collect in a queue, which keeps them in order until they can be serviced.

If many users share printers, at times demand temporarily exceeds printer capacity. It would waste users' time to refuse print jobs until a printer becomes available, and it would waste printing time to force the printer to sit idle as the next user initiates a new job from scratch.

NetWare maintains print queues that store print jobs and release them to printers. A user can go on with work as soon as his print job has been stored in the queue. Printers receive new jobs from the queue as soon as they finish the last one.

You can configure NetWare queues in several ways. If one queue services several printers, jobs are sent to the first available printer. If two queues with different priorities are created for the same printer, rush jobs are placed ahead of less critical jobs. Print queues are configured by system administrators, but are often invisible to users aside from the slight delay that queue printing introduces to the printing process.

The vast majority of recent applications are available in network versions. In addition to understanding the multiuser characteristics of networks, most such applications understand the way to work with network printing. Some applications work directly with NetWare print queues. Most applications, however, print to local printer ports (such as LPT1:). The NetWare shell intercepts this print data and diverts it to the network.

Core Printing Services in Netware 2.2

Traditionally, NetWare has only supported printers that were directly attached to the server. This limitation meant only five printers could be supported by the network, and that those printers had to be reasonably close to the server.

Printers attached to the server are supported by the NetWare 2.2 *Core Printing Services*, which are installed optionally when NetWare 2.2 is installed. You can use a variety of console commands to configure printers and queues, and to assign queues to printers.

Print Servers and Remote Printers

The limitations of Core Printing Services frequently are too great for any but small networks. Recently, therefore, Novell introduced NetWare *print server* technology. Print server software can run on a NetWare server, a workstation, or a bridge, and can manage jobs for up to 16 printers. Additional print servers can be installed on the network if more than 16 printers must be supported.

The printers can be attached directly to the PC that runs the print server software, but they also can be connected as *remote printers* to any workstation on the network. Now printers can be located anywhere on the network.

2.2 If Core Printing Services are not enabled on your NetWare 2.2 server, you must use INSTALL to generate a new operating system. This process is beyond the scope of this book, and is a task recommended only for experienced NetWare installers. Consult the NetWare 2.2 Installation manual for instructions.

Print servers and remote printers can be implemented under Netware 2.x as an alternative to Core Printing Services.

3.11 Netware 3.11 does not implement Core Printing Services. All printing is accomplished by means of NetWare print servers.

Tasks

Creating Printers and Queues from the NetWare 2.2 Console

Purpose

If you print through Core Printing Services, several printer and queue management functions are available from the server console. This task teaches you to set up a printer from the NetWare 2.2 console.

Steps

1. Create a queue. The following example creates a queue named HPLASER :

   `QUEUE HPLASER CREATE`

2. Create a printer and specify the port to which it is connected. Note the following example:

   `PRINTER 0 CREATE LPT1:`

3. Then associate the printer with the queue as in this example:

   `PRINTER 0ADD QUEUE HPLASER`

Notes

After you configure a queue and printer, jobs directed to the queue are sent to the printer associated with that queue. The PRINTER number is in the range of 0 through 4. Each printer must be associated with a port. The easiest ports to configure are parallel printer ports, which are named LPT1:, LPT2:, and LPT3:. Parallel ports require no configuration options.

Create additional queues and printers as required. Be sure that each queue has a unique name, and that each printer has a unique number and port assignment. You need to create the queue only once. The printer definitions, however, are lost when the server is booted.

You may want to add the printer definition command lines to the server AUTOEXEC file. To do this, follow these steps:

1. Start SYSCON.

2. Select **Supervisor Options**.

3. Select **Edit System AUTOEXEC file**.

4. Add these lines to the AUTOEXEC file:

   ```
   PRINTER 0 CREATE LPT1:

   PRINTER 0 ADD QUEUE HPLASER
   ```

Creating Queues from PCONSOLE

Purpose

This task enables you to add print queues from the PCONSOLE menu utility.

Steps

1. Start PCONSOLE.

2. Select **Print Queue Information**.

3. Press Ins.

4. Enter the name of the new queue.

5. Quit PCONSOLE if desired.

Notes

If you are using Core Printing Services, you must attach the queue to a printer by using the PRINTER console command. See the preceding tasks.

Configuring a Print Server

Purpose

Unless you print via NetWare 2.2 Core Printing Services, all NetWare printing is controlled by a print server running on a server, a PC, or a bridge. All versions of print servers are configured in the same way with PCONSOLE. This task illustrates the configuration of a print server that supports these printers:

- A local printer named LASER1 attached to the print server

- A remote printer named MATRIX1 attached to a workstation

After you define a print server in this task, refer to the subsequent task to run the print server on your network as an NLM, a VAP, or an EXE on a PC.

Steps

1. Log in as a supervisor to the server to be supported by this print server.

2. Start PCONSOLE.

3. Select **Print Queue Information** from the **Available Options** box. The **Print Queues** box lists existing queues.

4. Press Ins.

5. Enter the first queue name: LASER1. After you press Enter, you return to the **Print Queues** box.

6. Press Ins.

7. Enter the second queue name: MATRIX1. After you press Enter, you return to the **Print Queues** box.

8. Press Esc to return to the **Available Topics** menu.

9. Select **Print Server Information**. The **Print Servers** box is displayed, showing any existing print servers.

10. Press Ins.

11. Enter the name of the new print server: PSERVER1. After you press Enter, you return to the **Print Servers** box.

12. Press Enter to modify the new print server. The **Print Server Information** box is displayed.

13. Select **Print Server Configuration**. The **Print Server Configuration Menu** is displayed.

14. Select **Printer Configuration**. A list of printers is displayed. All printers are named Not Installed at this time.

15. Highlight the selection for printer 0 and press Enter.

16. Complete the screen entries as shown in Figure 5.1. Press Enter in the Type frame to display a menu from which you can select the printer type. Press Esc to return to the **Configured Printers** box.

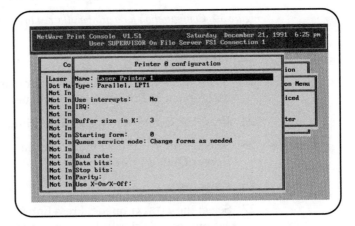

Figure 5.1: Configuration for a printer attached to a print server.

17. Highlight the selection for printer 1 and press Enter.

18. Complete the screen entries as shown in Figure 5.2. Press Esc to return to the **Configured Printers** box.

19. Press Esc to return to the **Print Server Configuration** menu.

20. Select **Queues Serviced by Printer**. The **Defined Printers** box is displayed.

21. Select printer 0 and press Enter to display the **File Server/Queue/Priority** box.

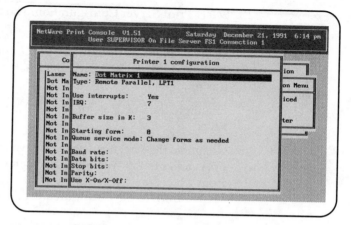

```
NetWare Print Console  V1.51                Saturday  December 21, 1991  6:14 pm
               User SUPERVISOR On File Server FS1 Connection 1

      Co                        Printer 1 configuration                    ion
   Laser  Name: Dot Matrix 1
   Dot Ma Type: Remote Parallel, LPT1                                      on Menu
   Not In
   Not In Use interrupts:       Yes                                        iced
   Not In IRQ:                   7
   Not In
   Not In Buffer size in K:     3
   Not In
   Not In Starting form:        0
   Not In Queue service mode: Change forms as needed                       ter
   Not In
   Not In Baud rate:
   Not In Data bits:
   Not In Stop bits:
   Not In Parity:
   Not In Use X-On/X-Off:
```

Figure 5.2: Configuration for a printer attached to a remote PC.

22. Press Ins.

23. Select the LASER1 queue. Press Enter to accept the assignment of Priority 1 to this queue.

24. Press Esc to return to the **Active Printers** box.

25. Select Printer 1. Press Enter to display the **File Server/Queue/Priority** box.

26. Press Ins.

27. Select the MATRIX1 queue. Press Enter to accept the assignment of Priority 1 to this queue.

28. Press Esc to return to the **Defined Printers** box.

29. Quit PCONSOLE if desired.

Notes

This task configured two printers, which differed in the following ways:

- LASER1 is physically attached to the print server. Its type is configured as Parallel, LPT1:. Usually you should not configure an interrupt for local printers.

- MATRIX1 is attached to a remote PC, and was assigned the type Remote Parallel, LPT1:. Remote printers must be configured with an interrupt. Interrupt 7 is normal for LPT1:.

Both queues were configured with a priority of 1. If you assign several queues to a single printer, the queues can have different priorities to control which jobs are printed first. Jobs in a queue with a priority of 1 print before jobs in a priority 2 queue.

To add several queues to a printer, insert them in the **File Server/Queue/Priority** box. A single queue can be assigned to several printers. Jobs sent to such a queue print on the first available printer.

Two queue options were not configured. To view these options, select **Print Queue Information** from the **Available Options** menu. Then choose a queue. The following options are displayed:

- **Queue Operators** can change the status of print jobs. The user SUPERVISOR is created as the operator for every queue. Add users and groups as required. Users cannot delete even their own jobs unless they are queue operators.

- **Queue Users** can place jobs into queues. Group EVERYONE is automatically installed as a user for every queue. Add or delete users and groups as required.

If a print server configuration is changed, the print server must be stopped and restarted before the changes can take effect. See the appropriate tasks for stopping and restarting your type of print server.

Starting **PSERVER.NLM** on a NetWare 386 Server

Purpose

After you define a print server, you can install it on a Netware 386 server by starting the PSERVER NLM. PSERVER.NLM requires 128K of server memory.

Steps

At the file console enter

LOAD PSERVER PSERVER1

Replace PSERVER1 with the name of a print server that you created using PCONSOLE.

Notes

After the PSERVER starts, the monitor displays a status screen, showing eight of the 16 available printers. Press any key to display the second eight printers.

Starting PSERVER.VAP on a NetWare 286 Server

Purpose

After you define a print server, you can install it on a Netware 2.x (version 2.15c or greater) server by starting the PSERVER VAP.

Steps

1. Copy the file PSERVER.VAP from the SYS:PUBLIC directory to the SYS:SYSTEM directory.

2. Down and reboot the server.

3. When the server prompts Value Added Processes have been defined. Do you wish to load them?, enter Y.

4. When the server prompts Print Server Name:, enter the name of the print server that was created in PCONSOLE.

Notes

The console command PSERVER STOP stops the print server. The console command PSERVER START restarts the print server. Use these commands to stop and restart a PSERVER.VAP so that you can install new configuration options.

Running **PSERVER.EXE** on a Workstation

Purpose

Any PC can run as a dedicated print server. Use this technique to reduce memory and processing demand on the server or when more than 16 printers are required. A basic PC with a single disk drive is all that is required.

Steps

1. To boot the PC from a floppy diskette, format a diskette with the /S option and copy the system files onto it.

2. Install a network interface card in the PC and connect it to the network.

3. Install IPX.COM and NETx.COM files in the root directory of the boot disk.

4. Copy the following files from SYS:PUBLIC to the root directory of the PC boot disk:

   IBM$RUN.OVL
   PSERVER.EXE
   SYS$ERR.DAT
   SYS$HELP.DAT
   SYS$MSG.DAT

5. Connect any local printers to printer ports on the PC.

6. Create a SHELL.CFG file in the root directory of the PC's boot disk. The file should contain the following line:

   SPX CONNECTIONS=60

7. Create the following AUTOEXEC.BAT file in the root directory of the PC's boot disk:

   IPX
   NET5
   PSERVER FS1 PSERVER1

Replace NET5 with the appropriate version of NETx for your boot diskette.

Replace FS1 with the name of the fileserver on which the print server was defined.

Replace PSERVER1 with the name of the print server that was defined in PCONSOLE.

8. Reboot the PC.

Notes

If the print server starts up correctly, a screen is displayed that shows the status of the first eight printers. Press any key to display the status of the other eight printers.

Checking the Status of a Print Server

Purpose

Use PCONSOLE to check the status of print servers.

Steps

1. Start PCONSOLE.

2. Select **Print Server Information**.

3. Select a print server from the displayed list.

4. Select **Print Server Status/Control**.

5. Select **Server Info**. If this option is not displayed, the print server is not active.

   The print server status information is displayed.

Downing a Print Server

Purpose

Any time you make a change to a print server, you must stop and restart the server. The safest way to stop a print server is through PCONSOLE because one option shuts down the print server only after current print jobs are completed.

To down a server, you must be the designated print server operator for that print server. Supervisors automatically are designated print server operators for all print servers.

Steps

1. Start PCONSOLE.

2. Select **Print Server Information.**

3. Select a print server from the displayed list.

4. Select **Print Server Status and Control.**

5. Select **Server Info.** If this option is not displayed, the print server is not active.

   The print server status information is displayed.

6. The **Current server status** field displays Running if the print server is active.

7. To down the server, press Enter. Then select one of the following options and press Enter to down the server:

   • **Down** downs the server immediately.

   • **Going down after current jobs** allows current print jobs to finish printing.

8. After the print server goes down, restart it using the appropriate method, as explained in the preceding tasks.

Notes

Note that you may experience difficulty with the **Going down after current jobs** option with printers that are temporarily halted. Printers that are out of paper, have been left off-line, or have malfunctioned may not go down. You must use PCONSOLE to stop the problem printers. After all printers finish their current jobs or have been stopped, the print server can go down. See "Controlling Printers on Print Servers" for information about stopping printers.

Starting a Remote Printer on a Workstation

Purpose

If you successfully install a print server, you can run remote printer software to enable workstations to support remote printers. This software runs as a Terminate and Stay Resident program (TSR) and requires 9K of memory. The workstation remains available as a regular workstation.

Steps

1. Connect a printer to the printer port of the PC. The port type must match the type that was configured for this printer when the print server was defined in PCONSOLE.

2. Edit or create a SHELL.CFG file in the workstation directory from which IPX.COM and NETx.COM are run. See Chapter 3 for a description of SHELL.CFG files. This file should contain the following line:

   PREFERRED SERVER=PS1

   Replace PS1 with the name of the fileserver on which the target print server is running.

3. Create the following AUTOEXEC.BAT file on the workstation:

```
ECHO OFF
CLS
PROMPT $P$G
PATH C:\DOS
C:
CD \NETWORK
IPX
NET5
F:
:LOOP
CLS
ECHO Attempting to initialize remote printer
connection
RPRINTER PSERVER1 1
```

```
IF ERRORLEVEL 1 GOTO LOOP
CLS
LOGIN
```

Replace PSERVER1 with the name of the print server that you defined in PCONSOLE. Replace 1 with the number of the remote printer on the print server to which this workstation should connect.

4. Copy the following files from SYS:PUBLIC to SYS:LOGIN on the workstation's preferred server:

```
IBM$RUN.OVL
RPRINTER.EXE
RPRINTER.HLP
SYS$HELP.DAT
SYS$ERR.DAT
SYS$MSG.DAT
```

5. Log out and reboot the PC.

Notes

See the next task for the method of checking the status of the remote printer.

The IF ERRORLEVEL line in the AUTOEXEC.BAT file checks the error return code of RPRINTER.EXE. If an error takes place, the batch file loops and tries again. Under some circumstances, several tries may be needed for the RPRINTER to connect successfully.

Directing Printing to a Network Printer

Purpose

To print to a network printer you must redirect printer output from a locally-attached printer to a queue servicing a printer attached to the fileserver or print server. Redirected printer output works with most applications that support LPT1, LPT2, or LPT3 printer ports and even works with the DOS Print Screen key.

Steps

1. Log in to the fileserver.

2. At the DOS prompt, type

   `CAPTURE LOCAL=1 QUEUE=LASER1 NB NFF NT TIMEOUT=5`

3. Load an application and make sure that the application is configured to print to the LPT1 printer port.

4. Start the printing process.

5. Exit the application, and type **ENDCAP** to disable the printer redirection.

Notes

CAPTURE redirects printed output from a local printer port to a network printer. The most important options for CAPTURE follow:

- QUEUE=*queuename* or Q=*queuename*. Replace *queuename* with a valid print queue name.

- JOB=*jobname* or J=*jobname* specifies that a print job configuration other than the default is to be used. See the tasks about print jobs for more information.

- LOCAL=*n* or L=*n*. You can use a 1, 2, or 3 setting with LOCAL= for LPT1:, LPT2:, and LPT3:. You can capture up to three queues at once by using separate CAPTURE commands. Applications can select among queues by printing to the corresponding port. If LOCAL= is not specified LPT1: is the default.

- TIMEOUT=*n* or TI=*n*. Use this option is to control printing from applications that are not NetWare aware. These applications do not send NetWare a command to print a job once it is completely in a print queue. The TIMEOUT option tells NetWare to close the job and print it if no data is sent within the number of seconds specified by *n*. If applications experience long pauses when printing, specify a high timeout value or the data is split into several print jobs.

If no timeout value is specified, you must exit non-NetWare-aware applications and execute the command ENDCAP to cancel CAPTURE and inform NetWare that the job can be printed. Usually you use the TIMEOUT option.

- NB instructs NetWare not to print the banner page with each job.

- NFF instructs NetWare not to send a form feed after the job is printed. Most applications send a form feed automatically, and a blank form is produced if NetWare also sends one.

  Leave this option out if you are printing screen prints or if you are printing from applications that do not send form feeds. Without the form feed, the next print job continues printing on the same page with the end of the current job.

- NT instructs NetWare not to convert Tab characters to spaces. This option is important if you are printing graphics. Under most circumstances, this option should be used with CAPTURE.

- NOTIFY and NONOTIFY tell NetWare whether to send a message to the user's PC after a job has been sent to the printer.

- CR=*filename*. This command instructs NetWare to print the job to the file specified by *filename*.

The command **ENDCAP ALL** ends redirection for all three LPT ports. The command **ENDCAP LOCAL=** followed by the port number disables printer redirection for the printer port. **ENDCAP LOCAL=2**, for example, stops redirection on LPT2 only.

Do not run ENDCAP until you finish printing.

To display the current print capturing status, enter this command:

```
CAPTURE SH
```

To capture a printer in a login script, precede CAPTURE with a # to designate it as an external command. Note the following example:

```
#CAPTURE LOCAL=1 QUEUE=LASER1 NB NFF NT TIMEOUT=5
```

You can capture different printers for users in different groups by placing IF statements in login scripts. Here is an example:

```
IF MEMBER OF "ACCT" THEN
#CAPTURE LOCAL=1 QUEUE=ACCT_LASER NB NFF NT TIMEOUT=5
END
```

In this way, each user can be assigned to a default printer at login.

Don't forget to include commands in your menu that enable users to change printers as required.

Printing Files with PRINT and NPRINT

Purpose

You can use the DOS PRINT and the NetWare NPRINT commands to print files through NetWare queues.

Steps

To print using DOS PRINT, follow these steps:

1. Enter a CAPTURE command with the desired options.

2. Use the DOS PRINT command. Printing to PRN: is the same as printing to LPT1:, and both work if LPT1: is selected in the CAPTURE command.

You can use NPRINT like DOS PRINT, but NPRINT accepts a number of options that make the use of CAPTURE optional. Here is a sample NPRINT command:

```
NPRINT SAMPLE.TXT QUEUE=LASER1 NB NFF NT
```

Notes

If you use NPRINT without options, the settings in your default print job are used. See "Making a Default Print Job Configuration" for more information about print jobs.

Here are some useful options for NPRINT that function like
the same options in CAPTURE:

- NOTIFY

- NB

- NFF

- NT

- QUEUE=*queuename*

- JOB=*jobname*

Listing and Deleting Print Jobs

Purpose

Users defined as queue operators can delete print jobs on
the queue by using PCONSOLE. Users defined as queue users
can list jobs but cannot delete them.

Steps

To list and optionally delete the jobs in a queue, follow
these steps:

1. Start PCONSOLE.

2. Select **Print Queue Information.**

3. Select a queue from the **Print Queues** list.

4. Select **Current Print Job Entries**.

   A list of jobs in the queue is displayed. The top job
   is the job that is currently being printed.

5. Highlight a job.

6. Press Del to delete the job. If you are deleting the
   current job, you must confirm your request.

Examining and Changing the Status of Print Jobs

Purpose

All users can examine print jobs on queues for which they are users. Users defined as queue operators can change the status or delete print jobs on the queue. PRINTCON is used for all queue management activities.

Steps

To list the jobs in a queue, follow these steps:

1. Start PCONSOLE.

2. Select **Print Queue Information.**

3. Select a queue from the **Print Queues** list.

4. Select **Current Print Job Entries**. A list of jobs in the queue is displayed. The top job is the job that is currently being printed.

5. Highlight a job.

6. To view information about the job, press Enter. The Print Queue Entry Information screen (see fig. 5.3) is displayed.

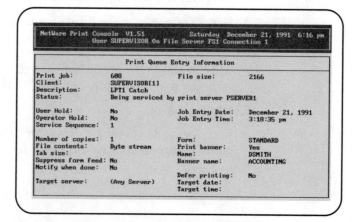

Figure 5.3: The Print Queue Entry Information screen.

7. If the job is not being printed, you can modify several fields on this screen. Change the fields and press Esc.

Notes

You can modify the following fields on the **Print Queue Entry Information** screen:

- **User Hold**. Change to **Yes** to hold the job in the queue. It is not serviced until the field is changed to **No**. The owner of the job can change this field.

- **Operator Hold**. Change to **Yes** to hold the job in the queue. It is not serviced until the field is changed to **No**. Only the queue operator can change this field.

- **Service Sequence**. Queue operators can change this number to alter the position of the job in the print queue.

- **Number of copies**. This field controls the number of times the job prints.

- **File contents**. This field indicates whether to treat the file as Byte Stream (don't convert tabs) or as Text (tabs convert to the number of spaces indicated by the **Tab size** field). Byte Stream is the most suitable setting in most circumstances. Selecting Byte Stream is equivalent to specifying NT (no tabs) in CAPTURE.

- **Tab size**. This field indicates the number of space characters that should print for each tab character in a Text file.

- **Suppress form feed**. If this field is Yes, no form feed is sent to the printer after the job completes.

- **Notify when done**. If this field is Yes, a message informs the user that the job has printed.

- **Form**. Use this option with forms created in PRINTDEF. Forms are discussed later in this chapter.

- **Print banner**. If this field is Yes, a banner page prints.

- **Name**. If a banner page prints, this entry appears in the name field.

- **Defer printing**. If this field is Yes, printing is postponed until the date and time specified in **Target date** and **Target time**.

Scheduling a Job for Deferred Printing

Purpose

If you want to print large jobs, you can delay printing until a time when few users are printing. Jobs can be held and scheduled to print at a specified time and date.

So that the job does not begin to print before you specify deferred printing in PRINTCON, configure a queue so that it accepts jobs, but does not allow jobs to be serviced by printers. The queue holds your job until you use PRINTCON to schedule a time for deferred printing. Then print the job to the queue and schedule it for printing at a specific time. Finally, release the queue so that it can be serviced by the printer.

Steps

Users must be designated as print queue operators for the queue to be used in order to complete all steps in this task.

1. Start PCONSOLE.

2. Select **Print Queue Information**.

3. Select a queue from the **Print Queues** list.

4. Select **Current Queue Status**.

5. Highlight the field **Servers can service entries in queue:** and change the field to No.

6. Quit PCONSOLE.

7. CAPTURE to the queue you have put on hold and print the desired job. Or use NPRINT to print the job.

8. Start PCONSOLE.

9. Select **Print Queue Information**.

10. Select the stopped queue from the **Print Queues** list.

11. Select **Current Print Job Entries**.

12. Highlight the job you want to delay and press Enter.

13. Change the **Defer printing** field to Yes.

14. Enter the **Target date** and **Target time** in the appropriate fields.

15. Press Esc twice to return to **Print Queue Information**.

16. Select **Current Queue Status**.

17. Highlight the **Servers can service entries in queue** field and change the field to Yes.

Notes

If you frequently defer printing, create a second print queue on the printer. Users will not use this queue for high priority jobs; therefore, the queue can be halted while deferred jobs are being entered.

Controlling Printers

Purpose

You can use PCONSOLE to control the status of printers that are connected to print servers. Users that are designated as print server operators can control the status of printers.

Steps

1. Start PCONSOLE.

2. Select **Print Server Information**.

3. Select the desired print server.

4. Select **Print Server Status/Control.**

5. Select **Printer Status.**

6. Select the desired printer. The status screen for that printer is displayed.

7. Press Enter to bring up a box that contains printer commands. The printer status screen with this box is displayed in Figure 5.4

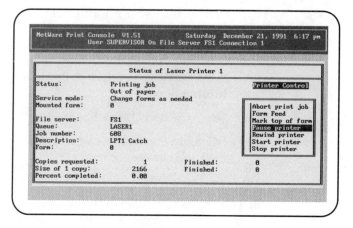

Figure 5.4: The Printer Status Screen command box.

8. If desired, select a printer command and press Enter. Or press Esc to exit to the status screen.

Notes

The Printer Status screen informs you of the printer's current activity. The printer waiting for a print server can be printing a job, out of paper, or may not be connected.

Remote printers that are not connected may need to have the RPRINTER program restarted on their host PCs.

The following commands can be issued to printers:

- **Abort print job** cancels the current print job and removes it from the queue.

- **Form Feed** sends a form feed command to the printer.

- **Mark top of form** prints a line of asterisks on the form to assist in adjusting the form position in the printer.

- **Pause printer** temporarily halts printing. If the print server is stopped and restarted, the printer is restarted automatically, and the current job resumes where it was paused.

- **Rewind printer** restarts printing from the beginning or from a specified number of bytes before or after the current point. Use this command if a malfunction has damaged part of the printout for a job.

- **Start printer** restarts a printer if it has been paused or stopped.

- **Stop printer** pauses the printer and returns the job to the queue. The job can be modified. When the printer is started, the first job in the queue is printed from the beginning.

Installing Printer and Form Definitions

Purpose

NetWare *printer definitions* work together with NetWare *print job configurations* to simplify printing on NetWare servers. Printer definitions contain a considerable amount of information about the various printers that may be installed on a network. Numerous printer definitions are shipped with NetWare; they can be found in the SYS:PUBLIC directory in files named *.PDF. Printer definitions are managed and modified with the NetWare PRINTDEF utility.

After printer definitions have been completed, they can be configured into NetWare print job configurations. In this task, you import the printer definition for a Hewlett Packard Laserjet III printer. You also can use PRINTDEF to create a standard form for use in defining print job configurations in PRINTCON.

Steps

1. Start PRINTDEF.

   The **PrintDef Options** box is displayed.

2. Select **Print Devices**.

3. Select **Import Print Devices**.

4. Enter the directory path SYS:PUBLIC.

   A box that contains a list of predefined printer devices is displayed.

5. Select the device entry HP LaserJet III. (Or substitute another printer from the list.)

6. Press Esc until you return to the **PrintDef Options** box.

7. Select **Forms**.

8. Press Ins.

9. Enter the following information in the fields provided:

Name:	Standard
Number	0
Length	0
Width	0

10. Press Esc. Quit PRINTDEF.

Notes

You can modify printer definitions with the **Edit Print Devices** option in PRINTDEF. You must understand printer configurations and control codes. Due to the variability of printers, editing of print devices is not considered in this book.

You should have one print form defined with the number 0; this is the default form number when defining print job configurations. The name does not matter. The Length and Width are for reference only and have no effect on printing.

Additional forms definitions can be used to halt printing on a queue until the mounted form has been changed, but you must assign someone to receive form change requests, to change the form on the printer, and to release the job in the queue. In most organizations, use of NetWare forms is inconvenient and is not recommended. If exactly one form is defined, no form change requests are generated. If your organization requires printing to several form types you should consider adding printers or obtaining multibin printers.

Making a Default Print Job Configuration

Purpose

Command lines for NPRINT and CAPTURE commands can grow rather long. If you use consistent combinations of options repeatedly, you can create a print job configuration. One print job configuration is your default, and it supplies options to NPRINT and CAPTURE automatically unless you override the defaults with options on the command line.

 Do not perform this task until you first complete the previous task "Installing Printer Definitions."

Steps

To create a print job configuration for printer LASER1, follow these steps:

1. At the DOS prompt, enter **PRINTCON**.

2. From the **Available Options** menu, select **Edit Print Job Configurations**.

   A list of any existing print job configurations is displayed.

3. Press Ins at the **Print Job Configurations** panel.

4. Enter **LASER1** at the **Enter new name** prompt.

5. Enter the configuration for LASER1. Suggested settings are shown in Figure 5.5. Modify these settings, particularly the queue name, to adapt the print job to your network.

The STANDARD form you created in PRINTDEF is entered automatically in the **Form** field.

In the **Print Devices** field press Enter and select the printer entry that was imported in PRINTDEF.

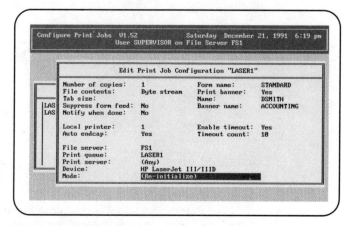

Figure 5.5: Sample Print Job Configuration.

6. Press Esc and answer **Yes** at the **Save Changes** prompt.

7. Press Esc repeatedly until the **Available Options** menu appears.

8. Choose **Select Default Print Job Configuration**.

9. Highlight the LASER1 configuration, and then press Enter.

   After you press Enter, (default) is displayed after the printer name.

10. Press Esc repeatedly and select **Yes** from the Exit Printcon menu.

11. Choose **Yes** at the **Save Print Job Configurations** prompt.

Notes

After you exit, the default settings are used every time you issue a NPRINT or CAPTURE command without switches.

Simply type **CAPTURE**. Then print a text file. Type **PRINT C:\AUTOEXEC.BAT**, for example. The file should print with the options defined in the default print job configuration.

In the print job configuration, the entry in **Device Functions** was left at (Re-initialize). This function resets the printer to its default options whenever you print. If the previous user left the printer configured for landscape printing, your default job returns it to portrait orientation if that is the printer's default.

Creating and Using Additional Print Job Configurations

Purpose

You can use print job configurations to control printer functions even when you print from applications that do not contain or control information for your printer. In this task, you create a job configuration that prints a job on a laser printer in landscape mode. You can use this job to print tables containing too many columns to fit on a vertical 8 1/2-by-11-inch paper.

Do not perform this task until you complete the previous task "Installing Printer Definitions."

Steps

To create a landscape print job configuration for printer LASER1, follow these steps:

1. At the DOS prompt, enter **PRINTCON**.

2. From the **Available Options** menu, select **Edit Print Job Configurations**.

   A list of any existing print job configurations is displayed.

3. Press Ins at the **Print Job Configurations** panel.

4. Enter `LASER1_L` at the `Enter new name` prompt.

5. Enter the configuration for `LASER1_L`. Suggested settings are shown in Figure 5.6. Modify these settings, particularly the queue name, to adapt the print job to your network.

   In the **Device Function** field press Enter. Select **Letter landscape, 45lpp, 12cpi**.

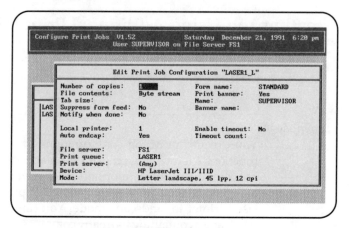

Figure 5.6: Landscape print job configuration.

6. Press Esc and answer **Yes** at the Save Changes prompt.

7. Press Esc repeatedly until **Save Print Job Configurations** prompt appears. Answer **Yes**.

Notes

To test the landscape printer configuration, use this example NPRINT command to print a file with the new job selected:

```
NPRINT C:\AUTOEXEC.BAT J=LASER1_L
```

The printout should be presented in landscape mode.

This technique has broad applications. Use it to control font sizes or to change the number of columns in printouts, for example. Different printers have different control options, and you may think of many ways to use this technique with your printer.

Copying Print Job Configurations to Other Users

Purpose

Printer definitions and print job configurations are stored individually in each user's mail directory. Each user has access only to the definitions he creates or that the supervisor copies to his mail directory. This task demonstrates the way in which to copy these definitions.

Steps

1. Log in as the supervisor.
2. Start PRINTCON.
3. Select **Copy Print Job Configurations**.
4. Enter the **Source User** id.
5. Enter the **Target User** id.

Notes

The target user must log in and use PRINTCON to edit the newly copied print job configurations and possibly to select a default print job.

After creating print job configurations, make sure that you exit PRINTCON and save the new print job configurations before you attempt to copy the configurations to other users. If you do not, the previous settings of PRINTCON are copied.

Sending On-Screen Reports to Printers

Purpose

You undoubtedly find times when you want to print the reports produced by NetWare utilities such as NDIR. To send these reports to a printer, use the DOS redirection operator.

Steps

1. Capture printing to the printer you want to use.

2. Request the desired report, but direct it to PRN: like this:

   ```
   NDIR *.DOC /UPDATE NOT AFTER 5-31-91 SUB C > PRN:
   ```

Notes

The > after the command is the DOS *redirection operator*. This operator directs any output that would have gone to the screen to the device that follows. PRN: is the same as LPT1:. If you want to redirect to LPT2: or LPT3:, then L=2 or L=3 must appear in the CAPTURE command.

Output can be redirected to files also. Just replace PRN: with a file path.

The C option instructs NDIR to generate continuous output, rather than pausing at the end of each screen. Without this option NDIR pauses after 24 lines have been sent to the printer. Because screen output is redirected, the prompt to press a key does not appear.

Nothing is displayed to the screen while the output is redirected; therefore, it is a good idea to make a trial run of the command to be redirected while you can see the output. Then you can be sure you receive the printed output you need.

6

COMMUNICATIONS

NetWare supports a rudimentary method of sending short messages to users. These messages appear on the twenty-fifth line of the user's screen.

This chapter discusses the following subjects:

- Sending messages to users and groups
- Sending messages to the system console
- Sending messages from FCONSOLE
- Enabling and disabling Message display

Tasks

Sending Messages to Users and Groups

Purpose

This task enables you to send brief messages to one or more users who are logged into the fileserver. The message displays at the bottom of the recipient's monitor unless that user is not receiving messages.

Steps

Use the SEND command to send a short message to other users. If, for example, you are a user named JJONES and you want to ask user DSMITH for his weekly reports, enter the following command at the DOS prompt:

```
SEND "Can I have your weekly report?" TO DSMITH
```

The user DSMITH then sees the following message at the bottom of his screen:

```
FROM JJONES[14] Can I have your weekly report?
(Press CTRL-ENTER to CLEAR)
```

In the preceding message, the [14] shows that this message was sent from station 14.

Notes

Messages can have a length up to 44 characters minus the length of your login ID.

To send a message to all logged-in users, send it to EVERYBODY.

You can send messages to groups or users. Specify GROUP or USER before the recipient ID if a user and a group share the ID.

Press Ctrl-Enter to clear messages from the screen. After you clear a message from the screen, you cannot recall it.

If several messages have been sent to a user, the messages are displayed one-by-one as the user presses Ctrl-Enter.

Messages sent to users who are not logged in are not stored. Users must be logged in and accepting messages before they can receive messages. Messages sent to users who are displaying graphic programs probably will not be displayed.

Sending Messages to the System Console

Purpose

This task enables you to send a message to the fileserver console.

Steps

Use the SEND command to send a message to the console. If you want to send a message to the console operator asking about the condition of the printer, for example, enter the following command at the DOS prompt:

```
SEND "Why isn't the printer printing?" TO CONSOLE
```

The message displays on the fileserver console.

Note

You do not need to clear messages sent to the console.

Sending Messages from FCONSOLE

Purpose

If you are going to shut down a Version 2.x fileserver from FCONSOLE, you may find it more convenient to broadcast a message notifying users of the shutdown from within FCONSOLE than from the command line.

Steps

 For this task, you must have supervisor rights or be a fileserver console operator.

1. At the DOS prompt, type **FCONSOLE** and press Enter.

   The **Available Options** menu is displayed.

2. From the **Available Options** menu, select **Broadcast Console Message**.

3. At the **Message** prompt, type the message you want to broadcast. Press Enter to send the message.

   The message text displays at the bottom of your screen and is broadcast across the LAN.

4. Press Ctrl-Enter to clear the message from your screen.

5. Exit **FCONSOLE** if desired.

Disabling and Enabling Message Display

Purpose

When a NetWare message is received on a workstation, all processing on the workstation freezes until Ctrl-Enter is pressed. If you are executing a long task that you don't want halted, you may want to turn off message reception.

Steps

To disable messages, execute the command **CASTOFF**. This command disables messages sent from users, but allows console messages.

To disable all messages including console messages (sent from FCONSOLE), execute the command **CASTOFF ALL**.

To reenable messages, enter the command **CASTON**.

Notes

Although you may be tempted to leave messaging turned off permanently, CASTOFF ALL should be used cautiously because it prevents you from receiving notification of system problems or of an impending server shutdown.

7

MONITORING
THE SERVER

A network fileserver can be extremely dynamic. User demand patterns can change almost overnight, and a server that had adequate capacity only a few weeks ago may not be approaching its limits.

This chapter discusses the ways in which you can monitor the server so that you can avoid potential problems and anticipate future requirements. Specifically, this chapter discusses the following topics:

- Monitoring NetWare 2.2 System Resources

- Monitoring NetWare 3.11 System Resources

- Viewing the Fileserver Error Log

- Switching a NetWare 2.2 Server between Console and Workstation Modes

- Removing DOS on a NetWare 3.x Server

Key Concepts

If you are a network administrator, you should get into the habit of checking your servers' health every day. By doing so, you will receive early warning of impending problems and you will begin to get a feel for usage trends, which will help you anticipate future requirements.

In addition to needing more disk storage, servers demonstrate their growing pains by demanding more memory. Additional users, workstations, and files demand more server memory.

2.2 NetWare 2.x servers have several static characteristics that are determined when you run INSTALL.

The number of *communications buffers* is determined by the operating system. You must generate a new operating system to change this value. That procedure is not covered in this book. Consult the NetWare 2.2 Installation manual for instructions.

You can alter the following characteristics by updating the fileserver definition as described in the Appendix of this book:

- Maximum open files
- Maximum open index files
- TTX maximum transactions
- Maximum bindery objects

Remember that Value-Added Processes use server memory. You may need to add memory if you are running a lot of VAPs.

3.11 Netware 386 dynamically allocates most memory as resources change their demands. You can correct most memory shortages simply by adding memory.

If you increase the system memory to over 16M, you need to add a REGISTER MEMORY command to the AUTOEXEC.NCF file. Consult the *System Administrator* manual for details about this command.

Tasks

Monitoring NetWare 2.2 System Resources

Purpose

The FCONSOLE command is the primary tool for monitoring NetWare 2.2 servers. This task suggests some things to examine in the FCONSOLE displays.

Steps

To monitor statistics in FCONSOLE, follow these steps:

1. Start FCONSOLE.

2. Select **Statistics**.

3. Examine the various statistics screens.

Notes

Pay particular attention to the following fields in the FCONSOLE statistics. Other entries are described on the FCONSOLE help screens, which you can access by pressing F1.

 FCONSOLE statistics are not available for NetWare 3.x servers. Instead, use the MONITOR loadable module.

Note the following fields in the Cache Statistics screen:

- **Dirty Cache Buffers**. Dirty cache buffers are buffers that are waiting to be written to disk. If this number is high or climbs, it may indicate that your hard disks' performance is insufficient. Some PCs that have been pressed into service as network servers do not have the fast disk subsystems that are often required for multiuser servers.

- **Cache Hits/Cache Misses**. Cache misses indicate the number of times NetWare attempted to read data from disk and could not find the data in the disk cache. If cache misses are consistently a significant fraction (over 5 to 10 percent) of cache hits, your server probably needs more memory.

- **Physical Read Errors** and **Physical Write Errors**. You should find zero or very few errors of this kind. These errors indicate hardware problems in your disk subsystem, and may forewarn a hard drive failure. Have the entire system examined by competent technicians.

- **Thrashing Count**. This field indicates that NetWare failed when attempting to allocate a new cache block. The operating system had to write the existing buffers to disk before it could read new data. Thrashing can seriously degrade server performance and is an almost certain indication that additional memory is required.

- **Hit on Unavailable Block** indicates that a request to read or write a cache block had to wait because the block was being updated to or from disk. High numbers here may indicate that your hard disk is not fast enough to keep up with the traffic on your server.

Note the following fields in the File System Statistics screen:

- Any FAT errors are an indication of problems with your hard disk. These errors are not necessarily fatal because NetWare maintains two copies of the FAT. If these numbers start to climb, check them frequently.

- **Fatal FAT Write Errors.** These errors indicate that NetWare failed when it attempted to update a copy of the FAT on the hard disk. NetWare can continue to use the in-memory copy. If the server is shut down, however, the disk-based FATs may be corrupted. Back up the server and obtain technical support!

- **Peak Indexed Files Open**. This number should always be less than **Configured Max Indexed Files**, or access to indexed files suffer.

Examine the LAN I/O Statistics screen and note especially the many fields that remain at or near a zero value. If the value of one of these fields begins to climb consistently, a problem may be degrading your network's performance. This type of problem, however, cannot be diagnosed without special equipment.

Note the following fields in the File Server Statistics Summary screen:

- **Current Server Utilization**. This field shows you how much horsepower remains in your server. Do not expect to run your server at 100 percent! If utilization is consistently above 60 to 70 percent, you should consider upgrading your server or splitting users onto additional servers.

- **Disk Requests Serviced from Cache** summarizes the Cache Hits/Cache Misses ratio from File System Statistics. This percentage should remain consistently high.

- **Unused Server Memory** is the amount of system memory (in megabytes) that is not permanently allocated. If this number falls, the system requires additional memory.

- **Dynamic Memory 2** is the only dynamic-memory option that is user-configurable. If the peak use approaches the maximum memory for this category, use the procedure in the Appendix of this book to increase the **Maximum Open Files** parameter.

Note the following fields in the **Transaction Tracking Statistics** screen:

- **Peak Transactions**. The number shown in this field should be smaller than **Configured Max Transactions**. Use the procedure in the Appendix to increase the configured maximum transactions.

- **Requested Backouts**. This field shows you how many times an incomplete transaction was backed out. This can be done at the request of an application, but may indicate network problems.

- **Unfilled Backout Requests** indicate that a backout request was not carried out. Such is the case if the TTS system has been disabled.

Monitoring NetWare 3.11 System Resources

Purpose

Statistics for NetWare 3.x servers are displayed in the MONITOR utility.

Steps

To display the Netware 3.x MONITOR, enter the command **LOAD MONITOR** from the NetWare console.

Notes

The initial Information screen displays the following performance statistics:

- **File server utilization**. This field shows you how much horsepower remains in your server. Do not expect to run your server at 100 percent! If utilization is consistently above 60 to 70 percent, you should consider upgrading your server or splitting users onto additional servers.

- **Dirty Cache Buffers** shows the number of cache buffers that have not been written to disk. If this number remains high, a very high level of file read/write activity may be indicated. Consider obtaining a faster hard disk subsystem.

The LAN Information screen enables you to display information about each LAN driver in the server. The specific statistics vary with each driver. Some statistics display error conditions. Others indicate data volumes and can be an aid to distributing traffic evenly if you have several cards and drivers installed in the server.

The Resource Utilization screen enables you to track memory use of all system resources. The screen displays the following performance statistics:

- **Permanent Memory Pool** is the amount of system memory that has been allocated for long-term use. Once allocated, this memory is not released until the server is booted.

- **Alloc Memory Pool**. This is the amount of memory that can be allocated for short-term tasks. This memory is used by the operating system for short-term tasks and is used by NetWare loadable modules, and is returned to the pool when the module is unloaded.

- **Cache buffers** shows you how much memory can be allocated for caching data. Novell recommends that you add memory if this figure falls below 20 percent. You can free memory for cache buffers by dismounting volumes or by unloading NLMs. Also consider removing DOS (see the task on removing DOS).

- **Cache Movable Memory** and **Cache-Non-Movable Memory** are other categories of temporarily allocated memory.

- **Total Server Work Memory** indicates the total memory that is available to NetWare.

The **Tracked Resources** box enables you to display the memory utilization of any of the listed resources.

Viewing the Fileserver Error Log

Purpose

System administrators should review the fileserver error log periodically, particularly if problems have been experienced. The following task shows you how to view this log.

Steps

1. Start SYSCON.

2. Select **Supervisor Options**.

3. Select **View File Server Error Log**.

4. Use the arrow keys to review the log. Press Ctrl-PgUp and Ctrl-PgDn to move to the beginning and end of the file.

5. Press Esc when you are done.

6. Respond to the Clear Error Log prompt by selecting **Yes** or **No.**

Switching a NetWare 2.2 Server between Console and Workstation Modes

Purpose

Users on a nondedicated server should not leave their workstations at the DOS prompt when they are not using the network. This slows the performance of the network for other users. If a nondedicated fileserver is left at the DOS prompt, up to 70 percent of fileserver resources are used just to manage this workstation, which leaves 30 percent of the fileserver's resources to be split among the remaining users. If the nondedicated fileserver is switched back to console mode, nearly 100 percent of its resources are available for other users.

Steps

1. To switch from DOS to console mode on a nondedicated server, enter **CONSOLE** at the DOS prompt.

2. To return to the DOS prompt on a nondedicated server, enter **DOS** at the : prompt.

Notes

The option of having a nondedicated server may have been valid when server-quality PCs cost several times as much as NetWare. With the decline in PC prices, however, the price of NetWare equals or exceeds the cost of a PC that can function as a server for a small department. It now makes greater sense, therefore, to run NetWare on a dedicated server rather than suffer performance degradation that affects all users on the network.

Removing DOS on a NetWare 3.x Server

Purpose

When memory is tight on a NetWare 3.x server, you can release some memory by removing DOS.

Steps

Enter the console command **REMOVE DOS**.

Notes

After DOS has been removed, the server no longer returns to DOS after the EXIT command. Instead, the server reboots. If the AUTOEXEC.BAT file executes the SERVER command, the server automatically restarts.

After DOS is removed, you no longer can edit STARTUP.NCF, which is a DOS file. If STARTUP.NCF is on the C: drive, you can boot the server with a boot diskette. If STARTUP.NCF is on a diskette, the diskette can be edited on another PC.

A

APPENDIX

Complete instructions for configuring a NetWare 2.2 server are beyond the scope of this book. New installation involves not only the installation of the server hardware, but entering of the hardware information into the server configuration. If you are uncomfortable with the procedures involved, you should have a qualified NetWare technician complete the initial server setup.

After the server is running, however, most users can reconfigure several of the server's operating characteristics. The process is straight forward, and there is little risk of damage to data or hardware.

Reconfiguring NetWare 2.2

Several tasks in this book describe parameters that system managers may need to alter, and this appendix refers you to the tasks for more detailed discussion. Other parameters are more easily explained, and they are discussed here.

You easily can alter the following system characteristics:

- **Server name.** This name can be from 2 to 45 characters selected from the following options:

  Letters A through Z

  Digits 0 through 9

  !, @, $, %, ^, &, (,), -, and _

  Period (.), provided it is not the first character

  Spaces may not appear. The underscore character (_) is frequently placed in names to give the appearance of a space.

  Generally speaking, server names should be short because you type them frequently. They should also be descriptive so that they make sense to users who must access several servers.

- **Maximum open files**

- **Maximum open index files**

- **TTS backout volume**

- **TTS maximum transactions**

- **Limit disk space**

- **Maximum bindery objects**

- **Install Macintosh VAP**

You can alter other settings, but some changes destroy the data on the affected drives or volumes. Any changes you make to partition or volume sizes are hazardous.

Modifying the following items destroys data:

- Hard disk logical size

- Partition Information, End

- Partition Information, Megabytes

- Volume Information, Megabytes

- Volume Information, Dir Entries

The procedure for changing the File Server Definition is simple. You must have a bootable DOS diskette as well as a working copy of the NetWare 2.2 System-1 diskette. Because the server must be brought down for a few minutes, plan your maintenance with due consideration of your users' access requirements. Disasters can happen, and you may want to schedule the reconfiguration for a time when you can reinstall NetWare and restore files from tape without disrupting your users' schedules.

To reconfigure the server definitions of a NetWare 2.2 server, follow these steps:

1. Make a tape backup of all server data. Although this procedure is not essential if you are changing nonhazardous parameters, it does ensure that you can recover from accidental loss of data.

2. Down the server by typing the following command at the file server console:

   DOWN

3. After the server is down, insert a bootable DOS diskette in the A: drive and power the server off and on to reboot. After the server boots, go to a DOS command line.

4. Insert the System-1 diskette and enter **INSTALL -F**.

   The -F is important because it instructs INSTALL to start midway into the installation process, at the point where file server definitions are entered.

5. The next screen you see should be the File Server Definition form. You can use the arrow keys to move to the various fields on the form. The form is taller than one screen, and you must move down to reveal its bottom portion.

   Highlight the fields you want to change. Press Enter to start the change. Then type the new field value and press Enter to end the change.

   Avoid making changes to fields that could damage data. INSTALL warns you that any changes to these fields can cause data loss and asks you to confirm the changes.

6. After you make all changes to the form, press F10.

   A box named **Actions to be Performed** is displayed.

7. If changes were made to the server definition, the next box will contain one or more action descriptions.

   - If any changes were made, the box displays the following information:

     `Replace Track Zero Information`

   - If you requested installation of the Macintosh VAPs, this action appears:

     `Install Macintosh VAPs (Value Added Process)`

8. Press Enter so that INSTALL will carry out the actions displayed.

You can select additional actions by pressing Ins and selecting the actions from the list that is presented.

You can remove an action by highlighting the action and pressing Del. If you delete the `Replace Track Zero Information` action, none of your changes go into effect, although Macintosh VAP still is installed if that action is requested.

9. Follow any instructions `INSTALL` may issue to the screen. You may be asked to change diskettes.

10. When asked to insert a diskette containing `COMMAND.COM`, you can power off the server, remove any floppy diskettes in the drives, and reboot it. This procedure completes the process of reconfiguring the server definition.

Index

D

T

New Riders Puts You on the Cutting Edge of Computer Information!

AUTOCAD

Inside AutoCAD, Special Edition	$34.95
AutoCAD: The Professional Reference	$39.95
AutoCAD Reference Guide, 2nd Edition	$14.95
AutoCAD Reference Guide Disk	$14.95
AutoCAD Student Workbook	$39.95
AutoCAD Instructor's Guide	$175.00
AutoCAD for Beginners	$19.95
Inside AutoCAD, 6th Edition Disk	$14.95
Maximizing AutoCAD, Volume I: Customizing AutoCAD with Macros & Menus	$34.95
Maximizing AutoCAD, Volume II: Inside AutoLISP	$34.95
Managing and Networking AutoCAD	$29.95
AutoCAD 3D Design and Presentation	$29.95
Inside AutoCAD Release 11, Metric Edition	$34.95

GRAPHICS

Inside CorelDRAW!, 2nd Edition	$29.95
Inside AutoSketch, 2nd Edition	$24.95
Inside Autodesk Animator	$29.95
Inside Generic CADD	$29.95

OPERATING SYSTEMS/NETWORKING/MISC.

Maximizing MS-DOS 5	$34.95
Maximizing Windows 3	$39.95
Inside Novell NetWare	$29.95
Inside LAN Manager	$34.95
Inside SCO UNIX	$29.95
Inside CompuServe	$29.95

NRP
NEW RIDERS
PUBLISHING

For More Information, Call Toll-Free
1-800-428-5331

New Riders Gives You
Maximum AutoCAD Performance!

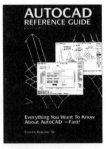

AutoCAD: The Professional Reference

New Riders Publishing

This is the most comprehensive desktop reference to AutoCAD commands and program features! Organized according to drawing tasks, the text includes examples for using commands. It also provides tips and warnings for increasing efficiency and troubleshooting problems.

Releases 10 & 11

1-56205-025-7, 1,000 pp., 7⅜ x 9¼

$39.95 USA

AutoCAD Reference Guide, 2nd Edition

Dorothy Kent

All of AutoCAD's commands and features in one quick, easy-to-use manual! Beginners and veterans will benefit from command explanations covering prompts, tips, and warnings. Filled with illustrations and practical examples.

Through Releases 10 & 11

0-934035-02-4, 288 pp., 5½ x 8½

$14.95 USA

Companion Disk
0-934035-84-9, $14.95 USA

More AutoCAD Titles from New Riders

AutoCAD 3D Design and Presenation
AutoCAD Release 11, AutoShade 2.0, Autodesk Animator 1.0, & 3D Studio

0-934035-81-4, 640 pp., 7 3/8 x 9 1/4
$29.95 USA

AutoCAD for Beginners
Releases 10 & 11

1-56205-015-X, 400 pp., 7 3/8 x 9 1/4
$19.95 USA

AutoCAD Student Workbook
Release 11

1-56205-018-4, 400 pp., 7 3/8 x 9 1/4
$39.95 USA

AutoCAD Instructor's Guide
Release 11

1-56205-024-9, 200 pp., 8 1/2 x 11
$175.00 USA

Inside AutoCAD, Special Edition
Releases 10 & 11

1-56205-020-6, 1,072 pp., 7⅜ x 9¼
$34.95 USA

Companion Disk
1-56205-030-3
$14.95 USA

Managing and Networking AutoCAD
Releases 10 & 11

0-934035-85-7, 432 pp., 7 3/8 x 9 1/4
$29.95 USA

Maximizing AutoCAD, Volume I: Customizing AutoCAD with Macros & Menus
Releases 10 & 11

0-934035-56-3, 432 pp., 7 3/8 x 9 1/4
$34.95 USA

Maximizing AutoCAD, Volume II: Inside AutoLISP
Releases 10 & 11

0-934035-98-9, 720 pp., 7 3/8 x 9 1/4
$34.95 USA

NEW RIDERS
PUBLISHING

To Order, Call:
(800) 428-5331 OR (317) 573-2500